Position Trading

Market Timing Mastery — Trade Like a Hedge Fund Manager by Discovering How to Spot Trends and Knowing Exactly When to Buy & Sell Your Stocks for Maximum Profit

Written By

Alpha Bull Traders

Alpha Bull Traders

© *Copyright 2019 Alpha Bull Traders- All rights reserved.*

The following eBook is reproduced below with the goal of providing information that is as accurate and reliable as possible. Regardless, purchasing this eBook can be seen as consent to the fact that both the publisher and the author of this book are in no way experts on the topics discussed within and that any recommendations or suggestions that are made herein are for entertainment purposes only. Professionals should be consulted as needed prior to undertaking any of the action endorsed herein.

This declaration is deemed fair and valid by both the American Bar Association and the Committee of Publishers Association and is legally binding throughout the United States.

Furthermore, the transmission, duplication or reproduction of any of the following work including specific information will be considered an illegal act irrespective of if it is done electronically or in print. This extends to creating a secondary or tertiary copy of the work or a recorded copy and is only allowed with express written consent from the Publisher. All additional right reserved.

The information in the following pages is broadly considered to be a truthful and accurate account of facts and as such any inattention, use or misuse of the information in question by the reader will render any resulting actions solely under their purview. There are no scenarios in which the publisher or the original author of this work can be in any fashion deemed liable for any hardship or damages that may befall them after undertaking information described herein.

Additionally, the information in the following pages is intended only for informational purposes and should thus be thought of as universal. As befitting its nature, it is presented without assurance regarding its prolonged validity or interim quality. Trademarks that are mentioned are done without written consent and can in no way be considered an endorsement from the trademark holder.

Financial Disclaimer:

I am not a financial advisor, this is not financial advice. This is not an investment guide nor investment advice. I am not recommending you buy any of the stocks listed here. Any form of investment or trading is liable to lose you money.

Accuracy Disclaimer:

All prices and market capitalizations are correct at the time of writing. Price and market cap information is sourced from official sources. All information in this eBook was derived from official sources where possible. Official sources meaning literature that is publicly available, provided by the company or official company website.

This eBook contains "forward-looking "statements as that term is defined in Section 27A of the Securities Act and Section 21E of the Securities Exchange Act of 1934, as amended by the Private Securities Litigation Reform Act of 1995. All statements, other than historical facts are forward-looking statements. Forward-looking statements concern future circumstances and results and other statements that are not historical facts and are sometimes identified by the words "may," "will," "should," "potential," "intend," "expect," "endeavour," "seek," "anticipate," "estimate," "overestimate," "underestimate," "believe," "could," "project," "predict," "continue," "target" or other similar words or expressions. Forward-looking statements are based upon current plans, estimates and expectations that are subject to risks, uncertainties and assumptions. Should one or more of these risks or uncertainties materialize, or should underlying assumptions prove incorrect, actual results may vary materially from those indicated or anticipated by such forward-looking statements. The inclusion of such statements should not be regarded as a representation that such plans, estimates or expectations will be achieved

Disclosure: At the time of writing, Alpha Bull Traders did not own shares of any of the stocks named.

Contents

Introduction 7

Chapter 1: What Exactly Is Position Trading? 15

Chapter 2: Best Trading Software 32

Chapter 3: Different Financial Instruments You Can Trade 47

Chapter 4: Fundamental Analysis 65

Chapter 5: Position Trading Indicators 78

Chapter 6: Identifying Momentum Stocks 91

Chapter 7: Hot Sector Mania 102

Chapter 8: Position Entry and Exit Strategies 116

Chapter 9: Money Management 130

Chapter 10: 7 Psychological Traps Every Trader Faces ... 136

Conclusion 142

Introduction

Gaining control over money is something that everyone in this world has pondered about at some point in their lives.

When it comes to the money that you have with you, you have a fair amount of freedom to decide on what you want to do with it. You can choose to save it. You can splurge it on getting that new car that has so many features, it might as well be the next Batmobile.

But imagine taking a large sum of money and placing it on an investment for a long time with the expectation that it will generate a profit. You cannot do anything you want with that investment. You cannot control it by nudging it towards the direction that you want it to go. It just follows the trends and eventually gives you a result after the period you have set for it. This is what position trading is all about, and despite how it sounds, more and more people are joining the ever-expanding world of trading.

Many amateurs ask, "Can someone make a living out of trading?" Since many so-called traders put their life savings on the line, the question seems pretty valid. Even if you are merely investing a small portion of your earnings, savings, or budget, it is still your money. So, there is no easy way to answer the question. Yes, you can earn big in trading; with enough successes, it might just seem like you are in the process of turning it into a career path. On the other hand, the path to success is a difficult one. In fact, it might just be one of the most difficult paths to take to make a living.

We have to constantly put ourselves in a position where we are going to face psychological discomfort and stress. And let's not forget the monetary stress that comes from knowing that your money could disappear forever, never to return to your hands again. Think of trading like the act of rowing downstream. You cannot control the river, but you can control your rowing. The world of trading is the river, and the act of rowing is you getting a control over your mind and emotions.

It may sound frightening, but the rewards are equally big. If you play your cards right, you won't have to work for an entire year while making your dreams of traveling come true.

So, what do we do in order to get good at the game of trading?

Before we find out an answer to that question, there is something that you should know: there is no secret technique or a get-rich-quick method for working on trades. The people who have gotten good at trading aren't using shortcuts, or the latest magic system they bought from some guy on the internet. They worked on their skills, learned from their mistakes, and kept evolving until they were good at what they do. They eventually developed strategies that helped them understand how to trade effectively.

So, what you need is not a secret technique but a consistent structure and a strategy that you can use to successfully understand the trading game and make informed decisions.

In fact, do you want to know what sets trading pros apart from the rest? You might be rather surprised by the results. Here they are:

- Great traders are opportunists. If they notice others reacting uncontrollably, they take advantage of that fact and try to capitalize on it.

- They are always aware of the latest trends. In fact, they know about the new trading methodologies that dominate the market.

- They are well-versed in the fundamentals of trading. They understand that you need to build a solid foundation to become good at something.

- Headlines are important. But you must know how to interpret them. When you are trading, keeping a close watch on the headlines gives you an idea of what you should be doing with your trades.

- Most importantly, they don't dwell on their disappointments for long. To them, every disappointment is one way not to do things. They understand that every mistake puts them closer to the right way of trading.

- Professional traders usually have a few strategies that they employ when they trade.

Now, you might read the above statements and wonder if that is all there is to becoming a great trader. Shouldn't there be a line about how great traders are using a particular type of system that gives them access to incredible strategies for making easy money? While there are systems and strategies that can help you with your trades, there is no way to make *easy* money. By using the word "easy," I am referring to a trade that has minimal risk but gives you a big return without any challenges.

One of the things to realize when you get the opportunity to watch amateur traders is how much they do not embody the above statements. They are impatient to get in on a trade, they skip learning the fundamentals. It is possible for them to let their emotions get the better of them, which can lead to costly mistakes. They might completely lose track of the latest economic and political news that concern their trade and end up losing their money.

Let's try and see two scenarios.

In 2018, a financial analyst from Vancouver decided to take action on a volatile market (Malito, 2018). The 24-year-old earns $50,000 a year. He decided that perhaps it was time to strike rich. The next thing you know, he lost all his lifesavings (which was close to $100,000) on his trade.

That sounds rather grim. In fact, no one would like to be on the receiving end of that situation. For some, it might signal the end to a trading career before it's even begun. Your mind must have drifted off towards your life savings, wondering if you are going to lose all that money. Not so fast, I have another real-life scenario for you to consider.

In 2015, a trader made a big bet (Diaz, 2015). He hedged his chances on the probability that semiconductor firm Applied Materials ($AMAT) might just get to break new heights. As it turned out, he was right. He made a cool $1.74 million in two days. Of course, if his bet was wrong, then he would have lost $1.74 million!

The two stories above highlight something important: anyone can win or lose big in the trading game. The entire process does not have to be complicated. All it requires is a keen mind and a few profitable strategies. When you have the right strategies, you can set up a successful trading position, which in turn provides you with a lot of benefits.

- You deal with less stress compared to other traders in the market. Day traders usually face volatility and high risk of losing all their capital. Position traders are saved from both, though.

- When you are engaged in position trading, you are using a long-term strategy. Traders use these long-term strategies to keep their positions open for days, weeks, and sometimes even months. Other forms of trading devise plans that are focused on short-term results. This means that methods that are not focused on position trading are open to attacks from short-term risks.

- In a position trader, the traders do not remove their trades from the market, even when the market is heading in the other direction. The traders do not exit too early, unlike other forms of trading. For example, in day trading, people might end up pulling out their trades with a loss. When you are a position trader, your biggest tool is your patience as you wait for the right level to take the profit.

- Position trading has a very hands-off approach to trading, which is not the same when it comes to intraday trading where you are doing due diligence every day in order to avoid a monetary catastrophe.

In a position trading, one only has to periodically monitor the trading position.

Here's an example of how one works with position trading. In 1999, the firm of trader Jim Chanos had analyzed the activities of Enron, a popular energy company. While everyone else was hopeful about the company's rise. Predicting the growth of the company, Jim Chanos had a strong belief that it was lying about their position and financial status. Trusting his belief, his firm started a short position, which was essentially a move where assets were sold in order to generate a profit from the fall or dip in the value of the asset. Jim strongly believed that Enron was going to end up in a disastrous position. Of course, he held his position for more than a year. But eventually, his predictions came true when Enron filed for bankruptcy in 2001.

Just how much profit did Jim Chanos make because of his prediction, you ask? A whopping $500 million.

All it took was for Chanos to have keen insights, the right strategy in place, and of course, the ability to stay abreast of the latest information (and to interpret them as well).

In the case of Jim Chanos, he had the advantage of years of experience. But all of those advantages, skills, insights, and understanding of the market had a beginning, a foundation.

And that is what you are going to receive.

This book will give you the foundational structures to help you navigate the complex world of position trading. It will become your guide to slowly build up your confidence and discover strategies that you can implement on your trades.

But as I have mentioned before, there is no get-rich quick scheme or secret technique to achieve that. While these tools are here to help you, they are not going to be of any use if you do not take actions to implement them. You are still going to be the one making decisions and facing the risks. You are still the one who will have to get back up from losses, should they happen.

In fact, if you think that someone is promising you an easy method to make money quickly off position trading, then you can be certain that you are probably being hustled. Every form of trading, whether position or currency, carries its own set of risks. Sure, the levels of risks are different between trading methods, but so are the rewards and the frequency at which you can get them.

Welcome to the world of position trading where the right management of money and financial strategy will allow you to achieve profits from three to 10 trades a year.

Chapter 1: What Exactly Is Position Trading?

The world of trading has gone through numerous stages of evolution. Today, based on your financial goals, you can choose a strategy that works best for you or a trading form that matches the amount of time you can devote to it. The modern investor has numerous tactics in his or her investment toolkit that complements the strategy being used.

One of the tools available to investors is what we call position trading.

In position trading, traders hold on to their stocks for an extended period of time. It may last anywhere from a few weeks to even years, which makes position trading the opposite of day trading (in which decisions are made almost every day). To a position trader, short-term influences, financial news, and price motions are of no concern. They are focused on the bigger picture and long-term market influences. On the most fundamental level, position trading relies on long-term historical patterns and general trends. Traders use them to decide what trades they would like to work on.

The Power of the Pareto Principle

Many people know what the Pareto Principle, also known as the 80/20 rule is. It is a universal law used for a lot of projects and activities, from learning languages to managing. If you haven't heard of it, that's okay.

Essentially, the 80/20 rule states that you are going to get 80% of your results from just 20% of the effort you put into your work. In all honesty, the split of 80 and 20 is an approximation, but the general idea behind the rule is the same. If you are working well, then you are using a small percentage of your efforts to generate big results.

At this point, you may be wondering, "What does this have to do with trading? Does it mean that we might be able to generate most of the results of the trade by using 20% of our efforts?"

Yes and no.

While the 80/20 rule does apply to the process of trading, we are looking at something else. In particular, the stocks.

You see, 80% of the price movement of stocks happen on 20% of the days. This is in direct opposition to the fact that trades make extreme shifts frequently, such as on a daily basis. However, what happens during the remaining days when the price is not making extreme shifts?

It's simple, the market trends sideways. A market becomes a sideways market or experiences a sideways drift. When the latter takes place, then trades fall within a predictable range without resulting in any major or dramatic change.

But just because there are no major changes does not mean that the market has become stagnant. On the contrary, the market is still active. It just means that price shifts are not rising or falling beyond set parameters or levels. This makes the market very predictable. You know how high trade prices will rise and how low they will dip. There are no surprises. The level of ambiguity has just been lifted, even if for a temporary period. What it means is that decision making is much easier during a sideways market than other, more volatile, times in the market.

Why does this happen? What causes prices to change?

It has got everything to do with the principle of demand and supply. When more people begin to buy a particular stock than sell it, then this action increases its demand and reduces its supply, which in turn increases its prices. Conversely, if more people were selling trades rather than buying it, then that would increase the supply and lower the demand, creating a price drop.

The concept of demand and supply is one that many people are familiar with. However, the idea that traders would prefer one stock over another is a little too complex to understand. What makes a trade more demanding that others? Why does demand and supply keep on rising or falling? What is going on in the minds of the traders when they like a particular stock and dislike another? There are no easy answers for any of the questions about trader behavior. However, there is a basic understanding of the trader mindset and the relation that mindset has with stocks: the direction the price of the stock moves is an indication of how much value the traders think a company is worth. This eventually decides whether they are buying the trades or selling them.

Position Trading vs. Buy and Hold

Another term that you will come across quite often when you are trading full-time is the concept of buy and hold. Essentially, in a buy-and-hold strategy, you keep an investment for a long period, hoping that the price will rise over time. You typically pay less transaction fees and lower profit taxes, too. However, with those advantages comes the fact that you need to have a lot of patience to see the payoff from a buy-and-hold trade.

Position Trading

But wait a minute: that sounds rather familiar. It does oddly bear resemblance to another form of trading that we have mentioned earlier: position trading. Both strategies may just seem like twins with different names.

However, what separates the two is the degree of chance that one places into the trades themselves. When you are using a buy-and-hold strategy, you are basing your decisions on the long-term prospects and improvements of the company. You are looking at what it has planned. You try and see how bright the future of the company is. Upon noticing that it can make tremendous progress, you invest in its growth. You are not concerned about the volatility of the market or the economic changes that occur frequently in the market. You are looking at the vision of the company's leaders, their growth targets, innovation strategies, and other components of the company itself.

On the other hand, position trading takes into consideration various factors other than the company itself. It focuses on trends and changes. Think about the trading style of Warren Buffet, one of the most renowned traders who focuses on position trading. He believes in two key principles while trading; one is to have patience and the other is to understand the market. When you think about it, position trading does not seem all that different from buy and hold. However, you are ignoring one of the key components in

Warren Buffett's strategy: understanding the market.

Market understanding separates position trading from buy and hold. When you talk about the latter, you are placing your bets on an optimistic view of a company's future position. It is akin to having blind faith in a particular trade. In position trading, you are trying to understand the market as well.

Let's try to explain the idea with an example.

Assume that it is 2007, and you are looking at the value of Nokia. In that year, nearly half of all smartphones sold around the world were made by Nokia (Minds, 2018). iPhone barely existed back then and controlled a measly 5% of the global smartphone trade. By looking at the position of Nokia, you think about the future. You understood the company's goals and ideas. With the way things were going, there seemed to be nothing that could topple the dominance that Nokia had on the market. You feel truly optimistic about the brand's future and use a buy-and-hold strategy to predict that you are going to get a profitable return in 5 years.

Sadly, your predictions would have been disastrous. In less than 5 years, Nokia's market value had declined by 90%. If you had indeed hedged your future trades on Nokia, you would have been the owner of a losing stock.

Let us now look at what a position trader would have done. He or she would have looked at Nokia's position and see its immense growth. So far, nothing has differed from the strategy used by buy and hold. However, position traders also look at the overall market, including the performance of other brands.

For example, they do not look at iPhone's share in the market and think, "Bah! Just 5%? You cannot topple the Nokia giant, you Apple peasant! Go back and cry to your motherboard!" Rather, they might look at it and think to themselves, "Well, that's a 5% control of the market, which is a result of a rise that was a long time coming. Based on market factors, it seems like the iPhone may rise even more in the future. Plus, we are talking about Apple. They are known for their quality products. I feel like this phone — combined with the technology of Apple — might just change the game."

For position traders, the entire market is littered with valuable information. They consider all of these things so that they can arrive at the right conclusion. It is true that they cannot make the market predictable, but they are exerting the power of knowledge to make their decisions as concrete as possible. Here are a couple of statements to sum up the difference between buy-and-hold and position traders.

- Buy and Hold: Yes, I think this might happen in the future.

- Position Traders: Yes, I think this might happen in the future because of the following reasons.

Position Trading vs. Swing Trading

The term "swing trading" comes up in conversations about trading. However, the difference between swing trading and position trading is as obvious as night and day.

When you are a swing trader, you enter into positions and then exit them in time spans that extend to one or a few days. In fact, one way to understand swing trading is by thinking of it as a slower form of day trading where transactions occur on an hourly basis. Compared to day traders, swing traders look for the highs and lows in the price of a particular trade. When they look at such patterns, they are able to make predictions about the value of the trade. However, their predictions cannot be made for the long-term. They can use their knowledge for the immediate future, occurring within the next few days.

Think of swing trading is the slower version of day trading. When you think of it that way and compare it to position trading, the latter is like watching a snail move. There is going to be little progress in the present but come back later and you might find the snail (a.k.a. trade) in a different location. For those interested in Swing Trading, we have compiled a beginner's guide, which is also available on Amazon and Audible.

Retail vs. Institutional Traders

With the technology available today, getting into trades is not a complicated scenario. One can start trading with the push of a single button. Still, it does not mean that all traders are the same. There are some noticeable differences, especially when you consider the case between retail and institutional traders.

Let us examine both types of traders individually.

Institutional Traders

One of the most noticeable traits of institutional traders is that they are able to work with large trades. This is because they are typically backed up by a firm or entity that has a lot of capital to spend. Institutional traders also have access to various forms of trade that are not usually made available to retail traders, such as swaps and forwards.

Many times, institutional traders work with large volumes of shares. Because of this, they can eventually affect the share price of a security. By purchasing large volumes, they show that the demand for the security or trade has increased, thereby creating an effect on the value of the security.

Now, let us look at the other end of the spectrum and push the spotlight on retail traders.

Retail Traders

Retail traders often invest in futures, options, bonds, and stocks. Most of the time, retail traders work with lots (which are exactly 100 shares), but they can choose to work with any number at a particular time.

The trading amount that retail traders use in a transaction is small and often based on their budget. However, they do pay more transactional cost because they use brokers to make their trades.

Where institutional traders can impact the price of the security, retail traders do not have such power because of the low transactional costs that they have to incur.

The Bottom Line

Apart from the methodology used by institutional and retail traders, there is also a difference in the thought processes between the two.

Retail traders are often prone to strong reactions because of their emotions. On the other hand, institutional traders are focused on taking actions. They want to remove the emotion from the equation and work with logic and information.

Retail traders can forget to understand the importance of mastering the basics. Institutional traders, meanwhile, realize that their level of expertise is based on the fact that they need to master the basics.

Retail traders are concerned about their losses. To them, each loss is a major setback. Institutional traders can afford to make losses since they are backed by institutions that have large finances.

Now that you know about the two different types of traders, you might wonder if there are special times during the day when you can trade. There are, and we are going to learn more about them.

During Open Hours vs. Aftermarket Trading

The people who are introduced to the world of trading know that stock market trading hours are from 9:30 am to 4:00 pm, Monday to Friday. Every day, billions of trades are conducted in the American stock market alone.

However, what most new traders won't realize is that the

stock market is open even after the market session has ended. This means that traders can work from 4:00 pm to 8:00 pm. This time frame is known as the aftermarket trading hours.

But is there a difference between trading during session hours and after them? Does it impact the trades in any way? It actually does.

During open hours, the markets deal with billions of transactions. Things only change when the market session closes. During the after-hours sessions, only a small percentage of the total volume of trades are being worked with. This means that traders have to think about their strategies even more in comparison to when they were trading during regular hours. The real question, however, is whether one can make money when trading in the aftermarket hours, considering they now have to work with limited trades.

The truth is that they can, but they might have to perform thorough research first. Here are some things to think about.

Company Announcements

When companies release information about themselves, such as their performance or financial earnings, they need to be strategic about it. If they release the information during market working hours, then it might cause traders to take impulsive actions — since quick decisions mean getting in on the action early — that might not take into account the true value of the stock of the company. This results in some serious repercussions. Let us take an example to explain this scenario.

Assume that the company announces their latest earnings, and they are worse than the last quarter. This can cause traders to impulsively move out of the stock so that they can minimize damages. However, it has a detrimental effect on the company. Because of the move-out, the company might suffer huge and unnecessary losses. In order to avoid such incidents, companies try to release announcements after regular working hours.

Now, check this: the value of the stock continues to move even after the market has closed because of the aftermarket hours. This means traders can access stock values that are often made public due to company announcements. They can use these values to make quick decisions about their stock. It is important because once the market reopens, the prices of the stocks have already changed, by which time those who had already taken advantage of the information received during the afterwork sessions have made the best use of it.

Now, that sounds pretty incredible. In fact, you might be thinking right now, "Why isn't everyone taking advantage of this system? Is this author telling me something that only an elite few know? Am I part of a high-society club and now has access to tons of information?"

Not exactly. You have to understand that not all companies release information after the market closes. Think of it as a gamble in which you are hoping that a company releases information for you to catch.

What's the Catch?

While you might have the advantage of information, there are some disadvantages to trading during aftermarket hours.

Among the biggest ones is that the market is much less liquid than trading during open hours. While you may have the advantage of time, you may not always have the benefit of liquidity unless it is a big move that has a major impact on a company.

Another disadvantage lies in the fact that there might not be a lot of people trading during aftermarket hours. This means that you might not be able to easily sell your stock.

Finally, if you discover that a company's earnings have dipped, and you would like to sell your stocks, then you might not be able to in certain cases, especially when you are dealing with smaller, non-blue-chip companies.

The biggest advantage to trading aftermarket hours, on the other hand, is that you are probably two or three steps ahead of everyone else in the decision-making process. Meaning, you can make a profit on news that you have been expecting for some time. Alternatively, you can decide if you would like to exit a stock if certain unexpected news gets announced. In the world of trading, being ahead in the game allows you to take effective decisions before the value of the stock goes in a particular direction.

No-Trade Zone

When talking about during trade hours and aftermarket, one might ponder if there is a situation where there is little or no trade on a particular stock.

That can happen indeed.

We refer to them as gaps, and they are sections on the chart where the price of a stock moves upwards on downwards sharply. These drastic changes have minimal or no trading in between. Why, you may ask?

For instance, we are under the assumption that a company's earnings are higher than expected. The company, in turn, chooses not to release this information during trade hours.

Rather, the news comes out during the aftermarketing trading hours. At that time, only a few traders are able to take advantage of the news. The next day, when the stock market opens, the company's stock might "gap up." Meaning, the stock price showed a much higher opening as compared to the closing on the previous day. Between the previous day and the morning of the new information, there is a gap in the charts.

Trading Lifestyle

One of the important things to note in position trading is to take your lifestyle into consideration. You need to plan your trades so that they can complement your lifestyle. You should not be changing it to match the trades because then you might face psychological and emotional stress.

When you are trading, you need to be in the right frame of mind. This allows you to focus and think with clarity, absorb all the information, and prevent you from jumping to conclusions about any trend. Sure, the stock might look like it is getting better, but is it the money-making breakout that you have been waiting for? Is it the stock that is going to get you enough money that you might retire on a private island of your own with a glass of martini in your hand? Or will it affect your finances so much that you might consider renting out your room on Airbnb to get back what you lost?

Even if losses occur, you should be in a state of mind where you are minimizing the degree of loss by creating your plan Bs and Cs. By doing this, you are not leaving anything to chance. You are creating alternatives and options so that you are prepared for anything. We will go more into depth later on in this book when we cover money management, portfolio allocation and exact numbers to be aware of when trading.

Even if you have been a buy-and-hold investor, and you are deciding to shift to position trading, it is always important to match the trade to your lifestyle. You may believe that buy and hold might seem similar to position trading, but it genuinely isn't. In fact, assuming that the two trading forms are similar might be your first mistake. You cannot simply transfer the strategies you have been using in buy-and-hold trading to position trading.

Chapter 2: Best Trading Software

Sometimes, you might come across people saying that a trader is often as good as the trading software that he or she uses. That might not be entirely true since your attention to details, ability to gather information, and general sense of awareness of the market are all important factors that come into play when considering your level of expertise. However, one cannot deny the huge impact that trading softwares have on the traders.

For many modern traders, a trading software is indeed their window to the world of trades. Softwares allow the trader to see patterns and trends. It allows them to make predictions, decisions, and investments.

You simply have to browse online to see the different softwares that are available for you to use. From independent developers to brokerage firms, you are going to find a plethora of options, each option providing you with their own unique set of features and options.

But then again, while browsing through all the different softwares available to you, you might notice that some softwares are meant for scanning while others are for trading.

So, what is a scanning software? Are they similar to a trading software?

Let's take a look into that.

Trading Softwares

With the growth of the internet and the connectivity it offers, there is an increase in the number of trading softwares. Additionally, with the easy availability of application development software, you now have trading software in popular application stores, such as iTunes and Google Play Store.

Trading software allow the users to trade and manage their trading accounts. They can make use of the various additional features like charts, forums, or even live economic news. All of them are provided to make trading easier for the users.

When you are looking into trading software, one of the most important decisions you will make revolves around what software is good for you. For example, some trading softwares provide automated features that might suit some types of traders. Apart from the features, you have to consider their fee structure, overall performance, analytical tools, and many other factors that match your trading style.

Scanning Software

A stock scanner or screener is a software that traders can use to filter stocks based on certain parameters. Scanning softwares come with free services (but with limited features) or with paid subscriptions (providing more advanced features). But regardless of what form of scanning software you choose, they both work with the same principle: they allow the users to find a trade based on a specific criteria or profile.

Let's take an example to show what scanners can actually do. If you are looking for a stock based on a specific price criterion, then you can input that criteria into the software and you will receive results of trades that match that criteria. This can be done with other parameters that include average volume, market capitalization, price change percentage, and various other criteria.

Some scanners also allow you to search for trades based on technical analysis data. For example, you can look at a particular data and choose if you would a stock to be above a particular level or below it. This helps you to plan out where you would like to enter your trades and how you would like to exit them as well.

Many traders often use the above method to find trades that look like they are going to perform better over a long period of time (which is essential for position trading).

By analyzing numerous stocks at the same time, traders can

weed out those trades that do not match their requirements.

Best Online Brokers

Now that we know the difference between trading software and scanning software, let's see if we can narrow down the best online traders or brokers that are available right now.

TD Ameritrade

Apart from the fact that TD Ameritrade has gained a reputation and following over the years, the platform is ideal for beginners who are starting their journey on a trading platform. It provides beginners all the necessary information to make important investment decisions. This is complemented by the fact that you receive numerous educational materials that guide you through the usage of the software, understanding the market, tutorials on making trade, expert advice, and lots more.

Charles Scwab

One of the features that traders will appreciate about Charles Schwab is the fact that you can start your account with $0 investment. In other words, there is no minimum amount required to open your account. Additionally, people who trade heavily might appreciate the $4.95 trading costs, which is lower than many of the softwares in the market.

Similar to TD Ameritrade, you can find numerous educational and research materials on Charles Schwab, allowing both beginners and professionals to learn something new from the platform. Additionally, traders can discover a variety of commission-free Exchange-Traded Funds (ETFs) that might appeal to many traders. ETFs are generally cheap trading options that are available to investors if they are choosing to build a diverse portfolio of investments.

E-Trade Financial

The thing that sets E-Trade Financial form the competitors is the fact that they are not just offering one app, but two different apps to cater to a wide variety or traders. In one of the apps, you can move money using a special feature called the mobile check deposit, giving you greater access to your funds. The other app is an acquisition made by E-Trade, which allows you access to a greater number of trades (as the second app is older than the first).

Ally Invest

Just like Charles Schwab, Ally Invest is opting to attract users with the $0 minimum account balance. This allows a wide variety of people to enter into the market. Another similar option that it shares with Charles Schwab is the low commission structure of $4.95 on stocks. But rather than become your typical broker, Ally Investment provides you with other options, such as forex trading, apps to manage your portfolio, and additional features for technical investors.

Full-Service Brokers and Discount Brokers

Even when you are choosing the right broker among the options available to you, you might also want to consider whether you would like to understand the difference between a full-service and discount broker.

Here are the major differences:

Features	Full-Service Brokers	Discount Brokers
Brokerage	They usually charge commissions based on a percentage value that is dependent on the terms of each trade that you execute.	They avoid the percentage model. A flat fee is usually offered for each trade.
Services	They provide more than just the buying	You are simply given a trading

	and selling of stocks. You can receive financial advisory features, retirement planning, and feedback on your portfolio among many other features.	platform for working with your stocks. No additional services are provided by the broker.
Fee Structure	Because of all the additional features mentioned above, you are charged a higher fee. Usually, you are charged 1-2% fee based on the assets you manage.	They usually do not have any additional charges because they don't offer the extra services that Full-Service Brokers do.
Trading Options	You get a whole lot of products such as options, commodities, forex, insurance, bonds, IPOs, and more.	You are mainly dealing with stocks and commodities.

Looking at the features of the two forms of brokers, it might be rather difficult for you to choose the right type of broker. However, you might consider using discount brokers for position trading. Here's why.

Lower Cost

Full-service brokers have higher costs and extra fees, which might not be suitable for those who are not comfortable shelling out a lot of cash on a trading platform. Another way to think about this is that the people who are planning their retirement or future goals might not want to constantly spend extra money on fees. They would use the trading platform for the purpose they want to achieve: trading. Because of the low commission's structure in discount trades, you often face low fee structures as well.

Unbiased Services

When full-service brokers offer advice, they might become biased towards a particular stock or trade. This means that they may try to sell you a particular stock more than others, not because it is necessarily good for you but because it is also in their best interests. You might not be able to catch on the sales tactics. Why would you? You did pay them to give you advice after all and for all intents and purposes — that is what they are doing. You might never think twice about what they are offering.

On the other hand, you have discount brokers. They do not provide you with advisory services. This is why they do not try to sell you a particular stock. Everything you see on their platform is a result of your own preferences and criteria.

Research and Information

While it is true that discount brokers do not provide any type of advisory features, they more than make up for it with the number of research and educational materials they provide. Typically, they cover a whole variety of topics. Because of the growing competition among various discount brokers, you might find many of them offering the latest news as well within the app. These news updates are available to you either through an updated feed or through video format (where they are connected to one of the many economic news channels around the world). This way, you might not even require an advisory service: you just have to compile all the relevant information and you have plenty of advice available for you.

Bottom Line

Choosing a discount broker works best for position trading. You are not investing too much into the platform. This gives you the freedom and peace of mind to focus on your trades. You might think that having advisory features might come in handy for you. However, this advice only tends to muddy the waters for you because you are unsure of whether you are being told to do something that benefits you or the broker.

Resources for Stock Scanning

Since we looked at some of the best brokers you can work with, it is now time to learn about a couple of scanning resources and just why you might need them.

Picture this scenario. You know what kind of watch you would like to get yourself. Perhaps it's a sports edition of a famous brand or one with the metal buckle. It could even be any type of quartz watch. Nevertheless, imagine finding yourself in a large showroom and left to your own without any guide and tasked to find what you were looking for.

That could be very well be the situation you might find yourself in if you enter trading. The only difference is that you are going to be replacing watches with stocks, trying to figure out just which stock is the best one for you to invest in a large stock market.

But imagine you had a guide who can help you navigate the complex world of stocks. All you have to do is figure out how much you would like to invest, the kind of stocks you are interested in, and voila! You have your options narrowed down and displayed right in front of you.

Doesn't that seem like a convenient way to enter into a trade? Rather than simply being inundated with information about so many trades that make feel like you are never going to start anywhere, why not have a few options to work with?

This is why you need a stock scanner. In general, almost every trading platform comes with its own version of a stock scanner. However, their version might be so rudimentary that you might not be able to get too much valuable information, or you might not be able to make accurate searches.

However, for that, you have another solution. You can make use of a stock scanner to get the right results.

So, having said that, are there any stock scanners that are recommended? Yes, there are.

ChartMill

This stock screener provides you with numerous tools that will aid you in your trading journey, which you can use to easily analyze and monitor the markets. With its innovative and detailed filtering capabilities, you will be able to conveniently filter through socks based on various criteria.

For example, you can filter your stocks based on sector and

price, allowing you to focus on the kind of companies you would be invested in. You can also choose the industry, giving you greater accessibility to choose a specific type of company.

Along with the filtering options, you also get the option of using charts. The charts have a clean interface that is easy to navigate.

Additionally, if you would like to check a stock further, you can make use of the stock analyzer. This tool gives you the capability to perform fundamental and technical analysis on a particular stock, giving you further details on the stock. This makes your decision-making process easier, and you have greater power to form your trading strategies.

Finally, if you are already interested in a particular stock, then you can easily find them using the search function as the tool lists each stock with their corresponding symbol.

Finviz

Finviz is another stock screener option for you.

With the screener feature, Finviz shines more than the other brands in the market. This is because of the easy-to-use interface that makes navigation smooth, even for first-time users who are quite alien to stock screeners.

One of the unique aspects of the platform is that you can

input the criteria yourself and receive every stock option possible that matches all or any of the criteria. You have even more search option tools on the platform, including options to search the prices based on market capitalization, outstanding shares, RSI, and even a specific candlestick pattern, which is a graphical pattern of showing the rise and fall of a stock. That last option is the standout feature of the platform because it allows you to use a particular strategy you have been building onto the platform and find stocks relevant to that strategy. However, the aforementioned search criteria are just some of the ones you can use. There are many more available on the platform that makes it easier for you to get the results that you want.

In short, you can have complete control over the stocks you would like to scan. You can even save your search criteria for later; in case you would like to go back to those options. When you have the ability to search for stocks based on numerous criteria and the capability to save your criteria, you are saving endless hours looking at your charts and backtracking to previous choices.

Finviz also provides you with heatmaps that show how valuable a particular stock is, as well as various charts that you can use to analyze your stocks. However, the downfall to the platform is its pricing structure. While you can use the free version, you won't be able to access all the best features and your screen is going to be littered with a whole lot of ads that is simply going to ruin the interface for you.

News Sources

Now that we focused on trading platforms and stock scanners, aren't we forgetting something? We are going to be making big financial decisions after all. Where are we going to get the information to make the right decisions?

From the news, of course.

So, does that mean you will need to be in front of your television set or laptop, looking through various channels until you find the right one?

Thankfully, that won't be the case if you have a platform that is dedicated to bringing you news about stocks, the market, and other relevant financial information.

Enter: Scoop Markets.

One of the things that makes Scoop Markets unique is that you can get all the news coverage about stocks and prices on one platform. It prevents you from mindlessly looking at multiple sources to find the information that you need.

You have a watchlist feature that allows you to add certain securities. Once done, you will start receiving information and updates about the security that you are focusing on right in your dashboard.

You can also look at any mergers and acquisitions, updates and recommendations from analysts, earnings reports, stock trades, and more. This allows you to get the right information at any time of the day.

One of the standout features of the platform is that you can even add certain topics to your feed, which gives you greater control over the news and information that you would like to receive.

They have both free and paid pricing levels. The forever free option lets you monitor up to 3 securities at a time, and is a great way to get a feel for the platform. Further paid options at $29/month and $69/month a month give you access to 25 and 75 securities respectively. Needless to say, just 1 good trade based on an alert from Scoop would return more than enough money to cover your subscription costs for the entire year. When starting out, you shouldn't need to monitor more than 25 securities, which makes the $29/month plan the ideal starting point for most regular position traders.

Chapter 3: Different Financial Instruments You Can Trade

Now that we have understood the various tools you can use to trade, let us now look at the securities that you are going to trade in. Starting off with the popular — and one that almost every trader is familiar with — stocks.

Stocks

A stock is also commonly referred to as "equity" or "share." It is a type of security that provides you with a portion of the ownership rights of the corporation that issued the stock. For example, if you bought the stocks of Samsung, then you have ownership rights based on the amount of stocks that you have in your hand. In addition, you are entitled to a proportion of the company's earnings and assets based on the value of the stock you are holding.

You will be able to get stocks predominantly in a stock exchange. However, that does not mean they cannot be sold privately as well. For the purpose of this book, we are going to be focusing on the things that are displayed on stock exchanges, considering they will also be available in the trading platform that you choose to use.

An important trait that you have to know about stocks is that transactions made on stocks should follow the rules and regulations set up by the government of the country the stock exchange is located in. This is done in order to protect investors and traders from fraudulent activities.

Now, the big question arises, "Why do companies raise stocks? The simple answer is that they require a certain amount of funds for either operating their business or for certain decisions.

What about ownership? How much ownership can one claim of a company?

Assume that there is a company by the name of ABC. This company has issued 1,000 shares in order to raise funds for a new technology that they would like to add to their operations. You decide to purchase 100 shares of the company, so you now own about 10% of the company's earnings and assets.

Does it mean that you can call yourself the owner of ABC?

When you purchase the stocks of a company, ou do get ownership rights where you are entitled to a portion of the company's earnings. However, you do not directly *own* the company. It is an important distinction that needs to be understood. The reason is that corporations and companies are treated like a person by law organizations. What this means is that corporations and companies have the freedom to own their own property, borrow money, face lawsuits if the situation does happen, and get other privileges that a typical person gets. This idea that a company is actually a "person" entails that the company is entitled to hold assets and even sell those assets whenever it wishes. In other words, anything that the company owns belongs to the company and not to the shareholders.

Understanding this distinction is important because most people come under the impression that they actually do own the company (or at least a part of it). So, before you go on Facebook and update your status as "Owner of Apple, baby!", understand that you are legally separate from the corporation and its intellectual and physical properties.

So, what happens to you if the company goes bankrupt?

Because the company is a separate entity from you, any case of bankruptcy does not affect you. You can actually still keep your shares with you. The only problem is that those shares might be worth nothing or the value might have dropped drastically after bankruptcy. This also works the other way around. When any of the shareholders become bankrupt, they cannot make use of the company's properties or assets to pay off their debts, as they are a separate entity from the company.

So, what does it mean when someone owns about 30% of the shares of the company? Does that make them powerful enough to take charge of the company? Not likely. Understand that it is wrong to say that one owns a third of the company because of the 30% shares. It is correct to say that one owns the entirety of a third of the company's shares.

Of course, by owning stocks, you do get to have the right to vote during the meetings held by the company. You are also entitled to the dividends of the company, based on the ahres you hold and when those dividends are distributed among the shareholders.

But what about those times when someone owns a major part of the company? Don't they technically own the company itself?

That is not true. This is the part where things get really tricky. What really happens is that the voting power of the person increases. Eventually, the person will be able to influence the board of directors of the company and even make a motion to replace them if he or she so chooses! This eventually changes the direction of the company, considering that having a new board of directors means that there is a whole new set of vision, objectives, and goals for the company.

For most shareholders, however, not being able to manage the company does not impact them greatly. They are comfortable owning a portion of the company's shares. It means that they receive a portion of the company's profits. The more shares you have, the more profits you receive. Essentially, profit-making is eventually the goal of these shareholders and power does not affect their decisions.

Another thing to note is the type of stocks.

Stock itself is divided into two main types. You have the common stock and then you have the preferred stock. When a shareholder owns a common stock, then he or she is entitled to receiving dividend and casting votes at company meetings. On the other hand, preferred shareholders do not have any voting rights. But they do have more priority over their dividends than those who own common stocks. In other words, when the company is paying out its dividends, it will first focus on the preferred shareholders and then move onto the common shareholders.

In this book, we are going to focus as the stocks as the security for position trading.

Exchange Traded Funds

A stock is a type of security. You can buy and sell it, but it is still considered as one type of security. On the other hand, Exchange Traded Funds (ETFs) are a collection of securities that is used for a particular index.

And what exactly is an index? Good question indeed.

An index (plural "indices") is a way to measure something. It is a hypothetical ruler or scale that can be used to indicate or measure the movement and performance of a price of practically anything. In the world of stocks and securities, it is used to measure the value of publicly traded goods. It does not focus on specific goods but rather an entire market or a segment of that market.

Let us take an example to highlight this.

One of the most popular indices in the world is the S&P 500. It collectively keeps a track of the performance and value of the top 500 companies in the United States. You cannot directly invest in an index. They are simply measuring tools to give you insights into stocks.

In order to work with index, you make use of ETFs. Essentially, an ETF holds the stocks that are part of a particular index or industry.

Going back to the previous example, we now know that you cannot buy from the index directly. However, what you have instead is an ETF named SPDR S&P 500 that has stocks of the companies of S7P 500 and keeps closed records and trackings of the S&P 500. You can purchase the ETF, allowing you to spread your stocks in numerous companies belonging to the S&P 500 index.

This is why an ETF does not hold one particular asset, such as the case of a stock. It actually holds multiple assets, which allows you to diversify your portfolio.

In fact, an ETF can hold on to more than hundreds of thousands of stocks scattered across various sectors and industries. Or it could even hold on to stocks that belong to a particular sector or industry. The eventual decision on which ETF to choose is based on the preferences of the trader and how much he or she is willing to invest.

Let us take another example to explain the point above now. If you were a trader, and you bought ETFs for the banking industry, then you would own stocks of various banks spread across the country.

Inverse ETFs

You can also make use of inverse ETFs. To understand that, let us get to know about how ETFs work. In a usual scenario, they make use of futures contracts to ensure that they achieve their returns. A futures contract is a type of contact where a trader decides to buy or sell a particular security at a specific price and time. This is done because futures securities allows traders to bet on the future outcome of a security. But they are not just predicting any outcome of a security. They are hoping the security or marker will rise in the future.

In an inverse ETF, the traders predict that the market will not rise, but will rather decline. If the market does decline — as predicted by the trader — then the value of the inverse ETF will rise by the same percentage that the value of the market drops. So if a market drops by 20%, the value of the ETF rises by 20%.

This is an important strategy, especially when it comes to bear markets.

Now, it brings us to another question: What is a bear market? Does it mean you are investing in some fine-looking grizzlies?

Not quite.

In the world of trading, you will come across two commonly used terms: bull and bear market. Understanding them is fairly simple. A bull market means that the market is on the rise. The prices are increasing, and there is optimism among the traders. The market is given the name "bull" because the animal usually attacks by raising its head up, and "up" is where the bull market goes.

On the other hand, a bear market represents the market that is going down. In other words, share prices are dropping and traders are pessimistic about the outcome. The market is given the name "bear" because a bear usually swipes down to attack.

If you look at the fact that the bear market is a decline in the prices of securities in the market, then it provides the perfect opportunity for people to take up inverse ETFs, given that they will profit from the decline in the market.

Cryptocurrency

A cryptocurrency is another form of currency, and it works like one as well. In truth, you can use it to make purchases, buy services, and perform transactions like any other form of currency that you use in your daily life. The only difference is that it is entirely virtual.

Cryptocurrency does not have a physical form and uses what is known as cryptography for its security. Because it is intangible and uses a complex security, it is difficult to counterfeit.

Most cryptocurrencies are not centralized. This means that they are not all regulated by one particular body, like a bank or financial institution.

What draws many agencies towards cryptocurrency? Is it the security features? Is it the fact that it is decentralized and not regulated by a financial authority? Could it be that one can create their own cryptocurrency provided they have the tools?

Actually, it's all of that, in addition to one more vital reason: it is organic.

What does that mean? Simply that is not issued by a particular body. In other words, it cannot be regulated by any government around the world. It is free of manipulation and interference from any governmental entity. It organically works with any organization because they can create a cryptocurrency of their own.

We are all aware of the first cryptocurrency to come out in the market and popularize the idea of cryptocurrencies: Bitcoin. However, that was just the beginning. Today, you only have to perform a cursory check online and you will discover thousands of alternate cryptocurrencies, each one with various features and functionalities. Some of the cryptocurrencies are clones; meaning, they replicate an existing cryptocurrency. The most common clones that you can find are those of the Bitcoin. Others are forks, referring to cryptocurrencies that are a variation of the original cryptocurrency.

Let us try to understand the example above. Assume that you have a cryptocurrency named Tradecoin. A clone would mean that someone out there created a cryptocurrency named Profitcoin, which is essentially the same as your coin. On the other hand, a fork would mean multiple coins created have more or less the same features as your coin but are not related to it. Let's say that Tradecoin 2 and Tradecoin 3 are variations of your coin, but they have some features removed or added so that they can appeal to a certain group of people.

Imagine going to a mobile phone showroom and looking at the latest iPhone. The attendant walks over to you and says that they have two versions of the phone: the 64GB version and the 128GB version. You are essentially looking at the same phone; you are only getting the freedom to choose between two different storage options. This concept of options is exactly what happens when a cryptocurrency has a fork.

Because of the decentralized nature of cryptocurrency, two parties can engage in a transaction without government scrutiny. However, cryptocurrency can be misused for various purposes, such as money laundering, purchasing drugs, and even tax evasion.

One of the ideas behind cryptocurrencies, apart from the high level of security, is that every transaction is recorded. A technology called blockchain uses a form of online ledger to store these transactions. Every new "block" on the ledger entry that is created has to be verified by all parties having access to the block. This means that if you are running a business with a couple of your friends using cryptocurrency, then every entry of cryptocurrency has to be approved by you and your friends.

However, if no transactions are supervised by governments, then how can anyone be certain that they are taking part in an official cryptocurrency deal? What guarantee does one have about the transaction that they are going to perform?

One of the ways this is possible is through the fact that many cryptocurrency transactions are a two-step process. This means that when you are about to make a transaction, you have to enter an authentication code. Once the code is entered, you will then have to confirm again whether you would like to go ahead with the transaction. This allows users to check and see if they are really interested and trust in the transaction before going ahead with it.

So, cryptocurrency seems like a profitable venture indeed. Surely, the disadvantages of dealing with cryptocurrencies could be minimal, right?

Not exactly.

One thing that makes it challenging to trade in cryptocurrencies is its incredibly volatile nature. In fact, it can be as volatile as 10 times the changes in prices as compared to the dollar. This means that you have the capacity to make 10 times the profit made using any other securities like stocks or bonds. But you also can make 10 times the losses.

The following factors cause the volatility of cryptocurrency.

- Geopolitical statements and events around the world affect cryptocurrency. For a regular currency, or fiat currency as they are called, it is affected by the country that owns that currency. In the case of cryptocurrency, news from anywhere in the world decides its future trends. This makes it highly unpredictable to see where the trend is going to go next.

- News stories that produce fear in the traders and investors also drive the value of cryptocurrency. Take for example the incident involving the closure of the online cryptocurrency platform Silk Road by the FBI (Greenberg, 2013) . The platform was a haven for all forms of illegal activities, including purchasing drugs, hiring hitmen, and money laundering. When people realized that the FBI would be getting involved in cryptocurrency dealings, their panic meter went into overdrive. They started abandoning their trades and distancing themselves for anything even containing the word "cryptocurrency."

With numerous factors are affecting cryptocurrency at once, it is no wonder that there is a lot of volatility to the currency. This is why the currency is never recommended for beginners because if you are not used to the cryptocurrency market, then you might end up making some huge losses. Those who trade in cryptocurrency is usually those who have been following the market for a long time.

Options

Options are basically instruments that you can use to buy or sell a particular asset. People can use options to deal with stocks, which is a type of asset.

What this means is that an option is literally what the term indicates: the option or choice to buy or sell a particular asset. When someone has options, they are not compelled to do a buy or sell transaction. It is entirely up to them to perform the transaction within a particular period of time.

You have two different kinds of options:

- The 'call' option allows you to buy your preferred asset at a particular price within a specified period of time.

- The 'put' option allows you to sell your preferred asset at a particular price within a specified period of time.

Each one can be attained by entering into a contract. The contract itself has an expiry date so the person who wishes to make use of the option must do so before the contract expires.

Let us look at the above security with the help of an example. Say that you are planning to get yourself an auto insurance (or any other type of insurance). You pay a monthly premium (or in some cases a yearly premium) for the insurance, which is valued much higher than the premium you pay for it.

Now, one year passes, but nothing has happened. It is time for you to renew your insurance. Even though you haven't used your insurance, you haven't lost much. This is because you had a peace of mind the entire year, knowing that any losses would be covered by your insurance. All you did in return was pay a nominal fee as premium. The only thing you have lost is the premium itself.

Think of the same idea for options. Rather than downright purchasing an entire set of stocks for a particular price, you take options. Just like how you don't exactly buy the entire insurance in one go, you are also not taking the entire stock in one go.

For instance, there is a stock of 100 shares available for $30 per share. That would mean that if you took 100 shares, then you will be paying $3,000 for those shares. Some people might find that a heavy investment. Instead, they purchase an options contract that is valued at $1.50 per contract. This means that 100 shares will be ($1.50x100) worth $150. So eventually, when you are trading, you will be trading based on your contract and its value.

With this, people will have the peace of mind knowing that they haven't actually invested a lot in the options, but they can still make a trade if they choose to.

Forex

Finally, we come to forex.

The term 'forex' is simply an abbreviation for foreign exchange. In other words, you are dealing with currencies instead of stocks of companies.

The currency exchange rate is what determines the

movement of ofrex. You will usually find these currencies quoted in pairs. The EUR/USD is a popular example of a currency that is traded in the forex market. But you can always find other examples such as GBP/USD or EUR/JPY.

So, what exactly decides the exchange rate of these currencies? Is there a body of organization that simply decides how much value a currency has based on arbitrary values? Or is there more to it than that?

What drives the currency of a particular country or nation is that country's economic, political, and other factors. Unemployment, trade deficits, inflation, geopolitical events, and the levels of industrial production are just some of the various factors that decide the value of a currency. This is why investors are always glued to their television screens for the latest news updates in order for them to make quick decisions about the currencies that they are dealing with.

With forex trading, you are making decisions every day. The forex market is a very liquid market. Most people make short-term strategies so that they can make as much money as possible in the short run.

The forex market also contains a high level of trading risk. It is this risk that one should think about before venturing forth into the forex market.

Alpha Bull Traders

The forex market becomes a source of information for position traders. When you are a position trader, you make use of the movement of other financial instruments — such as forex — to understand the value of your stock.

Chapter 4: Fundamental Analysis

Before you decide to analyze the stocks, you might come across a choice. You have to decide whether you would like to pick fundamental analysis or technical analysis.

Both forms of analysis have the same purpose: they are techniques that are used by traders and investors around the world to understand the stock market and make better decisions.

However, the key difference between them is how they operate and the type of data that they utilize to provide you with insights.

- On one hand, fundamental analysis aims to predict the prices of the stocks based on various industrial, economic, and company data and statistics. It also uses interests and dividends to make predictions about the stocks. It is almost like taking a birds' eye approach to data and statistics.

- On the other hand, you have technical analysis. This form of analysis focuses on the activity within the market. It uses internal market data to allow you to make your strategies and predictions.

But apart from the methods that are used by fundamental

and technical analysis, there are other notable differences as well. Let us look at some of them below.

Factor	Fundamental Analysis	Technical Analysis
Approach	Using various economic factors to predict the value of securities	Using the movements of prices and patterns on charts to predict the value of securities
Price Movements	It is focused on predicting the long-term movement of securities. This is why most investors who are using fundamental analysis are doing so to invest for a long-term. Because of this, they need to understand the numerous factors that could affect the movement of prices.	People who are using technical analysis are aiming for short-term price movements. They have strategies in place to buy and sell securities in the near future. A technical analysis becomes vital for securities such as forex, where transactions are conducted in the short-

		term.
Value of Shares	A fundamental analyst believes that there is an intrinsic value for each security and usually purchases that security when it falls below the intrinsic value. Using the same intrinsic value, he sells the security when its price goes above that value. Through this method, he or she makes a profit. Of course, finding out that intrinsic value means he has to use all the data provided by fundamental analysis.	A technical analyst believes in the fact that stocks don't have any particular value. He or she is of the opinion that only the forces of demand and supply can truly affect the prices of the stocks. THis is why, they avoid placing any particular value on the stock and simply base their decision on the direction in which the market is moving.
Trends	In fundamental analysis, people believe that there is no	Technical analysts are of the opinion that past trends may repeat over

67

	hope for using past trends or look for any sort of fluctuations in the prices.	time. They use historical data and chart information to find out if there is a possibility that there is a repeat of a past trend.
Assumptions	Fundamental analysts do not make any assumptions. They review their decisions based on the information that they have gathered from various sources that we talked about earlier.	Technical analysts make certain assumptions. One of the reasons for this is the idea that past trends can repeat again.
Decisions	To a fundamental analyst, there are numerous factors that are used to come to a decision. In many ways, the decision of a fundamental analyst	Analysts do not have any personal view of things. they are solely dependent on the direction of the market. To them, the market is the one giving the

	are based on his or her subjective opinions.	opinions.
Changes	Because fundamental analysis is based on long-term strategies and patterns, the indicators change less frequently than technical analysis. Usually, fundamental analysis indicators change on a quarterly basis.	Short-term strategies require frequent changes in indicators. You will notice that it takes weeks, days, and sometimes even mere hours to notice changes in indicators.

Need for Fundamental Analysis in Position Trading

Some of you might think that having technical analysis tools will suffice for making decisions. After all, you have everything you require to focus on the factors in the market. You feel that paying attention to the market is more important than considering what economic factors influence a company or a stock.

When you use fundamental analysis, though, you are not merely aiming to make predictions. You are looking at the overall performance and health of any company. Remember the passage regarding Nokia that we looked at earlier. If one were to simply use technical analysis, then the bigger picture of the rock might be ignored to look at the immediate position of the stock. However, if one had used fundamental analysis, then they would look at the stock from a broader perspective.

That is where fundamental analysis becomes important. It tries to answer some of the important questions that you might have about a company or stock, such as:

- Is it really true that the company is going to see a rise in revenue?

- Is the company capable of making an actual profit?

- Does the company stand a chance to beat the competitors in the future?

Like the questions above, fundamental analysis tackles many other queries that are important to understand where the market is going.

Apart from that, here are some other advantages of fundamental analysis.

Discovering Future Movement of Prices

Since you are using position trading to work on long-term strategies, you might need to have an idea of how the prices might move in the future. This movement will then help you decide whether you would like to invest more in a stock or whether you should be prepared to sell it. The one way you are going to gain an understanding of future price movements is through fundamental analysis.

Fair Value

Fundamental analysis plays an important role in finding out the company's fair value. This fair value helps you understand the company's present financial standing. This, in turn, lets you know the amount that has to be paid between parties if the stock of the company is sold in the market.

Management Evaluation

When you use fundamental analysis, you are also evaluating the management and trying to find out more about their internal decisions. It is similar to the forex market, where you evaluate an entire country so that you can understand what is going to happen to its currency. By knowing about the management of a company, you might be able to predict the direction the stocks might take as a position trader.

Competitive Advantage

When you use fundamental analysis, you are also finding out if the company you are focusing on has the ability to beat its competitors. This factor becomes important in determining whether the value of the stock you are holding will increase or decrease in the future. This is why, you need to ask yourself, "Is the company capable of growing to such a point that it can beat the competition?"

Financial Strength

It is always nice to see that a company is growing. Does that mean the company is financially strong, though? Is the company capable of paying off all its debts on time? One of the mistakes that traders make is that they do not conduct more research on the company before purchasing their stock. They look at the company's current value and position and think that it is poised for success. They miss out on seeing the financial capabilities and strengths of the company.

When you use fundamental analysis, you enter the market with all the cards on the table. You are not hoping that something will happen. You have an understanding of what might happen based on information available to you. In other words, your level or certainty increases.

Understanding Important Concepts

At this point, we are clear that fundamental analysis is important for position trading. But while you are working with fundamental analysis, you might come across certain terms that could stop you in your tracks and make you wonder, "Wait, what is this? What is it trying to tell me?"

Earnings Per Share

We use earnings per share to measure how much profit a company has earned. Typically, you might begin to notice that companies release their earnings per share data on a quarterly or yearly basis.

Essentially, earnings per share is a portion of the profits of the company that is allotted to each outstanding share.

Let us say that a company has generated a net income of $20 million. It now has to pay off the dividends of the preferred shareholders. Assume that the amount for preferred shareholders is $2 million and further assume that it now has 10 million shares that are outstanding in the first quarter of the year. In the next quarter, it has about 12 million shares that are outstanding. Based on the information provided, here is how we will calculate the earnings per share.

We first remove the amount already paid to the preferred

shareholders.

That would be:

$20 million - $2 million = $18 million

We can now use the remaining $18 million to measure the earnings per share.

Since it has 10 million shares outstanding in one quarter and 12 million in another, then it has an average of 11 million shares outstanding. An important note to make here. WE are calculating average to only measure the earnings per share of the company. We are not using it to show how many shares the company has to pay. If a company has 10 million shares outstanding, it has to pay all 10 million shares. The same rule applies if it has 12 million shares as well.

The next part is fairly simple. We take the amount it has right now — which would be $18 million — and then divide it by the number of shares outstanding.

Therefore, $18 million divided by 11 million shares.

This gives a value of $1.63.

In other words, the company's earnings per share is $1.63. In other words, it has earned $1.63 for each share investment made into the company.

Price-to-Earnings Ratio

The price-to-earnings (P/E) ratio is a way to evaluate the value of a company that uses its earnings per share to measure its current share price. In other words, you are establishing a relation between the company's stock prices and the earnings per share.

The P/E ratio is used widely to gain a better understanding of the value of a company. Earnings are vital to understand the health of a company because investors need to know the degree of portability of the company in the present and the degree of profitability it will attain in the future. Both of these factors help the investor understand how to use his or her money effectively.

Debt to Equity

The debt-to-equity (D/E) ratio is calculated by taking the total liabilities of the company and dividing it by the company's shareholder equity. One uses this ratio to find out how much financing the company has received from investors and creditors. When it is higher, then it means that the company has received a major part of its financing from creditors (for example, from banks). It's investor financing (from the issue of shares) is lower.

How is this ratio used?

If there is a high debt to equity ratio, then the company could be considered as a financial risk to many traders. This is because of the fact that when companies have high loans, then the losses suffered by the companies if they do not meet those loans are higher.

Traders do not want to risk their investments on a company that cannot maintain its debts.

Return on Equity

The return on equity is a ratio that measures profitability. This profitability measures the ability of the company to create profits from the investments made the shareholders in the company. In other words, traders can use this ratio to find out how much profit each dollar they invest in the company generates.

This ratio is not measured by the company. Rather, it is used by the investors to gauge the level of success of a company and how much they are going to receive for the investment they pour into the company. In other words, it is a way to evaluate how much profits trades can make and whether they are capable of getting their money back.

Cash Flow Ratio

All companies have certain degree of liabilities.

But the question is, "What is happening to those liabilities?"

This is what the cash flow ratio aims to answer. It simply aims to find out how well the company is able to manage its liabilities with the cash that is flowing into it through various operations and assets. This helps measure the liquidity of the company.

As you might have guessed, a cash flow ratio lets you know if the company is capable of managing its liabilities. This means, can it pay back its shareholders easily or is it going to face some roadblocks in that area? With that knowledge in hand, you are able to make more sound investment decisions.

As you might have guessed, a cash flow ratio lets you know if the company is capable of managing its liabilities. Meaning, can it pay back its shareholders easily or is it going to face some roadblocks in that area? With that knowledge in hand, you are able to make more sound investment decisions.

Chapter 5: Position Trading Indicators

Before you decide to analyze the stocks, you might come across a choice. You have to decide whether you would like to pick fundamental analysis or technical analysis.

Both forms of analysis have the same purpose: they are techniques that are used by traders and investors around the world to understand the stock market and make better decisions.

When new traders enter into the market, they are faced with understanding trade indicators. There is just so much information in front of you that making heads or tails of it might seem like a daunting task. In fact, many traders skip using the indicators and hope that they are able to gain their information from other sources.

But avoiding the indicators is not going to solve anything. Rather, it might just make your decisions riskier.

Let us start with technical indicators.

When you enter into the market, you are going to notice numerous technical indicators. You might ponder about which one you should consider or if all of them are important to you in some way. You look at each indicator and try to find out what they are trying to say in the hopes that one of them might make more sense to you than the others. But that is not the right way to go about things. There is an easier approach.

All you need to know is that most technical indicators give you the same set of information in different ways.

Many traders have already been in your position. They have experienced the same mistakes that you have made. This is why, it is better to learn from past mistakes.

Before we delve deeper into technical analysis, let us first try to understand two concepts that are commonly used in technical analysis. These two concepts are part of the chart patterns that you analyze.

Support

Support usually occurs during a downward trend in the price levels. As the prices continue to go down, there can be a pause in their progress because of a sudden surge in demand. As the price of securities continue to drop, an increase in the demand for the securities increase. The increase in demand acts as a support line for the ashes.

In a similar manner, a resistance occurs when there is an increase in the sell-off of stocks as the price is increasing.

Once traders have identified a certain "area" of of support or resistance, then it helps them with finding out where they would like to enter or exit the trade. When the price reaches a particular point that is either a support or resistance, then one of the two situations will occur: the price will hit the support or resistant point and bounce back or it might continue on its trajectory, in which case a new support or resistance point is established.

How does this work with trades?

Simple. Many trades are made on the prediction that the prices will not pass the support or resistant points. Other traders make predictions on the fact that prices will cross the aforementioned points. Either way, how you predict the market can determine whether it works in your favor or against you.

So, how does one decide the support and resistance levels? Let's use an example to find out.

We now have a trader named Andrew who saw that over the past few months, the price of these tock has not risen above $51. It has reached the $51 point repeatedly, but it has not managed to cross that mark yet. In such a scenario, $51 will be considered as the resistance point. This is made on the belief that the price won't go beyond that point. Based on this, traders can start making predictions on the price. If they decide that there is a possibility that the price might cross the resistant point, then they can modify their strategies accordingly.

Novice traders often make the mistake of selling into support because they begin to panic about the situation of the stock. They think that they are going to make a loss and make rash decisions. A smart trader will be looking for this opportunity and buy what the new trader has sold. Eventually, when the chart shows the price reaching into resistance, the experienced trader sells their stock and ends up making a lot of money. Novice traders also end up buying into support, thinking that the prices may rise even further in the future. This strategy is not based on any knowledge of the market but a general understanding of the mechanisms of support and resistance. Selling into support and buying into resistance are not always the most prudent courses of action to take.

Hence, it helps to understand various parts of a technical analysis.

200-Day EMA

One of the technical indicators that you might notice is popular in the market is the 200 -day Moving Average or 200-day EMA.

It is calculated by taking the average of a security's (in this case, a stock's) closing price across the last 200 days.

In other words, you take the average from Day 1, Day 2, Day 3, and all the way to Day 200. You then add the numbers together and finally divide that number by 200. Typically, you won't have to perform the calculations on your own as the platform you are using will provide you with the 200-day EMA by itself. However, in case you decide that perhaps you trust only yourself, then you now have the formula.

When you look at the 200-day EMA broadly, then you might automatically assume that as the average gets higher, the more it enters the bullish market. After all, an increase in the average means things are looking good right?

This is where novice traders make mistakes. They end up taking everything at face value without realizing how the market works. When there are high readings, it is considered as a warning by smart traders. While novice traders might think of this as an opportunity to buy stocks, smart traders realize that a big change is just looming over the horizon. When there are high readings, it means that traders are overly optimistic. There are not many new buyers in the market. This eventually causes the market to reverse and begin to head in the downward direction faster than you can say, "Wait, what just happened?"

50-Day EMA

A 50-day Moving Average or 50-day EMA is similar to the

200-day EMA. The only difference is that you are calculating the average over the course of a 50-day period rather than take into consideration 200 days. Even when using just 50 days, one has to realize that just because the average is getting higher and higher, it does not mean that the market it bullish. Try and find out how quickly the average is rising. Ask yourself if this makes any sense to you. Do not only look for optimistic results as that is a calamitous approach to take in a stock market.

Stochastic RSI

The Stochastic RSI is an indicator that makes use of the relative strength index (RSI) values. A Stochastic oscillator formula is used on the RSI values in order to get results that fall into the range of zero to a hundred.

- An RSI is an index that measures the momentum of price. This allows traders to evaluate those situations where the stock has been overbought or oversold.

- An oscillator, on the other hand, is an analysis tool that shifts between two extreme points. By using these points, it can create a trend indicator.

When you combine both factors, then you can understand that the Stochastic oscillator helps in finding out whether a particular RSI value is oversold or overbought. It appears by placing values between two oscillation points, zero and hundred.

The Stochastic RSI is using properties of two different factors to create an indicator that is highly sensitive to the price changes in the market. This is why most traders use it to evaluate the historical performance of a particular stock rather than use it for a general price analysis.

In other words, you are looking at the bigger picture instead of just what is happening to the price right now.

Getting a Clearer Picture of Technical Analysis

By using technical analysis, you are using a certain analysis discipline to perform an evaluation on the investments you own. This allows you to see trading opportunities and are usually depicted as patterns and trends on charts.

Because technical analysts believe that past trends can have a big impact on the price movements in the future, they are consciously looking at historical data to notice any patterns that they can use in their analysis.

Now, one of the things that you might wonder when looking at the charts during technical analysis is what exactly drives the patterns and trends. Is there an unknown force that no one can see that is secretly influencing the analysis? Is this an indication that the Illuminati exists and that they are influencing the stock markets secretly?

Well, before the paranoia sets in, let us clear up some misconceptions. All the numbers, patterns, and trends that you see on the charts are not arbitrarily decided. They are based on the decisions, predictions, and actions of human beings.

Let us take a small example.

When traders are optimistic about the market, they react accordingly. This causes the demand in the market to increase, which eventually causes the prices to increase. When you are using your 200-day EMA, you might notice that things are looking good. But does that mean it will continue to stay good? Eventually, there might be a downward trajectory of the prices in the market. Even the downward direction of the price is determined by human beings as well, as there are fewer buyers in the market. When you begin to understand the human logic that guides most of the patterns and trends on the charts, you realize that they become more predictable.

Suddenly, you see the charts with more clarity. You do not get intimidated by the big numbers and complex patterns either. You realize that it is all about cause and reaction. A reaction has a particular cause and you can usually trace back the patterns to that cause.

Now, you are probably feeling more comfortable approaching charts. That is good. After all, you do need to maintain a clear head if you would like to know more and start making important financial decisions.

When you first start looking at charts for technical analysis, then you might notice that there are options to choose the time frame. You can choose anywhere from one-minute time frame to a monthly time analysis to even years. The time frames that you choose to analyze depends entirely on your trading style. There are some popular time frames that many traders typically use, including

- 5 minutes
- 15 minutes
- Hourly
- 4 hours
- Daily

For example, if you are trading in the short-term, then you might consider using the 5- minute, 15-minute, or even daily charts to perform your analysis. However, if you are a position trader, then using small time frame is not going to help you out a lot. Besides, it might just bombard you with so much data that you are going to spend hours, and maybe even days, to go through all that data. It does not seem practical at all.

Rather, if you are focusing on long-term trades, you might want to analyze your data in month-by-month increments or even yearly data (if you are planning to keep you position open for long).

Another thing that you might notice — apart from the option to choose the time frame — is the option to use different kinds of charts for the purpose of technical analysis.

Let us look at some of the tools and indicators that one can use for technical analysis.

Trendline Indicator

Trendlines are a popular form of indicators in technical analysis. This makes sense since technical analysis focuses on the fact that the market can show trends (which is why they focus on past data in order to spot future trends).

You may not be able to find trends in the short run. However, as you look at charts over a period of days or weeks or even months, you might begin to notice certain patterns in the charts. These patterns can, in turn, be used to make predictions and strategies.

Hence, when you use a trendline indicator, you can get a possible direction for the price action. While the direction is also a form of prediction (as you might never be sure of what happens in the future), it is not entirely a guess. This is because that direction your find will be based on data and not random factors.

Support and Resistance

We have already understood what support and resistance can do for your technical analysis. One thing to reiterate here is that when a price action breaks the present support or resistant levels, then it usually continues onto the next or bounces away from the point it was heading for and move in the opposite direction. Make sure you are aware of this when you are planning to buy or sell stocks.

Moving Average Indicators

We have already seen two types of moving averages: the 200-day EMA and 50-day EMA.

In the grand scheme of things, it won't matter much if you do not have the required data to measure either the 200-day or the 50-day EMA. It is only when you have the measurements for either of the EMAs that you are able to get a clear picture of the market.

Additionally, you can also use the 100-day EMA and the 500-day EMA as well. Both of these indicators, when combined with the 50-day and 200-day EMAs, are going to explain the market to you properly. Never think that one particular EMA as the main source of information. Try and analyze the market using different approaches and see what valuable information you can find out about your stocks.

Bottom Line

Here is an important thing to remember: this book can help you find out about different technical analysis available to you. You might even be introduced to the concepts behind those analysis methods. However, you cannot use the concepts you have learnt here to perform technical analysis in detail. If you would like to learn more, then you need to delve into books that are specially made to help you navigate the various components of technical analysis.

If you would like to train yourself in the technical analysis methods, then you need to get yourself a book that will not only serve as a primer to the analysis but take you through the steps to learn more about it.

I personally recommend the book *Trend Trading For Dummies* by Barry Burns. The book is easy to browse through and provides you with step-by-step methods work with technical analysis.

I have noticed that many people are drawn towards *Technical Analysis for Dummies*. While many people might think that the two books can be interchangeable and that getting either of those books will help, do note that there is a vast difference between the books. For one, *Trend Trading for Dummies* slowly eases you into the concepts of technical analysis and gain mastery over it.

Now that we have gone over technical analysis, it is finally time to step into the realm of momentum stocks.

Chapter 6: Identifying Momentum Stocks

You have understood what tools you are going to require when entering the market. You have understood certain concepts that will help you when navigating the market. Now it is time to finally understand how to identify certain stocks. Most importantly, we are going to identify momentum stocks.

Still, what is momentum investing?

Momentum Investing

The main idea behind momentum investing is to capitalize on a particular market trend that is occurring continuously. It means that when securities start showing upward trends, then you are going to go long and when they start showing downward trends, then you are going to go short.

Now, you are probably wondering, "What does going long and going short mean?" Surely, it has got nothing to do with height.

It does not.

Going long can also be understood as having a long position.

This means that you own a particular security. When someone goes long, it refers to the act of continuing to own the security in the hopes that the value of the stock will rise in the future.

The opposite of going long is going short. When you are going short, you are holding a short position, which is indicated by the sale of a stock that you do not personally own. This means that the investor borrows a certain stock and sells it back to the lender. This is done in the hopes that the price of the stock will drop, and the investor can buy it at a low price.

One of the strategies used by investors in momentum investing is moving averages. The investors use one average that is shorter than the other average.

For example, the two averages one can consider could be the 50-day or 200-day moving average. When the 50-day average crosses the 200-day average, then it gives an indication to the investor to buy stocks. In the same way, if the 50-day average falls below the 200-day average, then the trader has to go for a sell strategy.

Momentum Stocks

One of the first steps that you will be taking is identifying the momentum stocks. You can use many criteria in order to identify these stocks. These criteria can be used on their own or in combination with other criteria. The main goal is to identify those stocks that are really experiencing a momentum in the market.

One trick that can be used here is entering the search criteria into a stock scanner. This will help you narrow down the potential list of stocks to find those that have momentum. Once you have the stocks ready, you can analyze them even more before you decide to trade using any one of them.

By using the below criteria, you will be able to find stocks that can easily go in an upward trajectory and increase in value by 30% or even 100% in just 3 months. Of course, you will have to do the legwork of researching more about the stocks you have with you and figuring out just which one those socks is going to give you the return you are looking for.

Earnings Growth

A common characteristic that you will notice in most, if not all, momentum stocks is that they are frequently showing a growth in their revenue and earnings per share. In many cases, momentums stocks tend to outperform the predictions set down by the analysts. So, how can you find out these stocks? Simple. You look for those stocks that have shown an increase in earnings per share from one quarter to another. You should ideally make sure that increases have happened in the past year. It would be even more advantageous for you if you can find stocks that have also shown an increase in their earnings per share in the most recent quarter when you compare it to the same quarter last year.

For example, if you notice that the earnings per share in Q1 (or first quarter) of a company in the year 2019 is higher than Q1 of the company in the year 2018, then you are probably looking at a momentum stock. But do not just jump to conclusions about the stock. Make sure that you are checking the growth in Q2, Q3, and Q4 of 2018 as well to get a better picture of the performance of the stock.

High Returns

In the short-term, it is quite easy to spot a momentum stock. There is no challenge in that endeavor. However, it then becomes rather difficult when you would like to know true momentum stocks. One can go about that by analyzing the prices of the stocks that are yielding high returns over the past three or six months. In fact, make sure that you measure the yield for the past year as well. You should compare the yields that you discover to some of the popular indices in the world (such as S&P 500). You should then see if the yield generated by your stock is higher than the indices that you are comparing the stock to.

New Highs

Another trait of momentum sock is that they are constantly setting new highs for themselves. It may not happen constantly, but over a period of time, you might notice that the company is always aiming to match the highs that they created and then break those highs., eventually creating a new target. This shows that the stock is on a constant upward trend. Some of these stocks might even increase by 30% or even 100% in a relatively short span of 3 months. Of course, the trick is to find these stocks in the market.

Remember that you should never assume anything when you can find information about it. The key motto that you should follow is: *The more you learn, the more you earn.*

If you are able to find information about something, then make sure that you have acquired that information. Do not simply assume something and hope that it is true. You might come across certain scenarios where you are not able to get any information. That is completely alright because you lack information. It was not because you did not try to get it, but it was unavailable to you for a reason.

Important Tips for Momentum Traders

Entering the market can be a daunting task. You have to figure out most of the way yourself. Even if you are going through hundreds of lessons and information, you are the one to eventually take action.

In fact, there is a big difference between knowing what you have to do and actually taking action to do it. Let us look at the example of practice sessions. Many traders use practice sessions and trading simulators to practice their trading game. They come up with a strategy that seems to work every time they use their simulation. However, once they begin to trade in real, they give up all their strategies and simply go in another direction entirely.

They had a winning strategy, but when it came to trade in real, the completely ignored that strategy.

This is always what happens when you have all the information and lessons. You might think you are prepared but when you enter into a trade, then everything changes.

Thus, here are some important tips that you can take with you when entering a momentum trade.

Do Not Get Attached to Stocks

A losing stock is a losing stock. Do not get attached to it and hope that it is going to change directions in the future. Do not try to bounce back with that particular stock.

Sometimes, it is better to cut losses and try a different avenue than stick to one particular stock than watch as your capital continues to dwindle away.

Do Not Try to Choose Bottoms and Tops

You are not here to identify the top of the trend or the bottom of the trend. Those are just assumptions. You are here to look at the trend and see where it is going to take you.

Make sure that you are sticking to the trend. In order to identify tops and bottoms, you will have to go through another set of analysis. Which is why, stick to the knowledge that you have about momentum stocks.

Be Confident

This might seem like an obvious trait for traders to have. After all, why go into trading is one is not confident about the trade? However, there are many traders who do lose their confidence as soon as they start looking at the numbers and the trends.

It is easy to get overwhelmed by all the date surrounding you. But the key thing to remember is that you need to focus on what you know. Do not try and take in all the information at once. That could overload your mind and even change your opinions about your trade. Simply look at the things you already know. Try to get your bearings straight. If there are numerous information available, then try to start with the one that makes the most sense to you. When you have identified one, then move on to the other. As you solve each part of the puzzle, you gain more confidence in your abilities and your knowledge.

Know When You Are Wrong

Do not cover your mistakes by trying to do something else. When you are wrong, take a moment to admit that you are wrong and see what happened. Analyze the mistake and see what went wrong and when.

As soon as you admit that you are wrong, you will stop wasting time on a trade that is not yielding the results that you want.

Remember That Results Take Time

You are a position trader. Do not be hasty when you do not see results for some time. You are playing for the long run. So, make sure you have your eye on the price and wait for the trade to pick up. If you notice that eventually, the trade is not working out for you, plan some strategies so that you know how much losses you are willing to bear before you pull out of the stock.

The Essential Concept

Professional traders are not impatient. They are calculating, and they wait for their turn to strike. Because of that, they typically buy after a wave of selling has occurred. This allows them to buy at the conditions that are suitable to them. Similarly, they sell after a wave of buying has occurred. During both the aforementioned scenarios, professional traders make sure that they have the right conditions to make a move in the market.

You see, when novice traders see a rise in the market, they react to it immediately. They think that they are going to miss out on some big action and decide to buy stocks. After all, buying them now and selling them later when the price is even higher, right? It seems like simple logic. Only, in the world of trading, nothing can be boiled down to simple logic. Professionals usually wait to see what happens in the market. Most of the time, they are selling their stocks and gaining what profits they can. This way, when the market eventually goes down, they can start buying stocks at the cheap. Rinse and repeat, and you have a strong strategy there. Of course, it is not always that simple, but it gives you an idea of what you should be doing when you notice a particular trend: do not look for the obvious.

Now let's take a look at one of the greatest momentum stock trades of all time.

George Soros

George Soros is often considered as one of the most successful traders in recent history. What elevated him to that position was a single trade that he conducted on September 16 1992 which would reap him an astonishing amount.

In the 1992, England was part of the European Exchange Rate Mechanism. This was a fixed-rate system that also included numerous European nations. The other countries realized that the value of the British Pound was high, and they put the pressure on England to devalue the currency so that it matches the strength of the other countries in the system. England, on the other hand, resisted the pressure for as long as it could, but eventually decided to float its currency. Soros saw what was going on and leveraged his firm against the pound, shorting it continously. Ultimately the Bank of England caved in, and stopped artificially propping up the currency, and eventually withdrawing it from the ERM. Betting against the Bank of England resulted in Soros netting an incredible $1 billion in a single day and cementing his reputation as the world's #1 currency speculator.

Benefit of 50-Day and 200-Day EMAs

As we saw earlier, the 50-day and 200-day EMAs are convenient if you would like to place a strategy to find out when you would like to buy or sell stocks. You use one average, which is the 200-day EMA average to place points on the charts. When you notice that the 50-day EMA crosses the 200-day EMA in a particular manner, then you can decide what you would like to do with your stocks.

In fact, in the world of trading, when the 50-day EMA goes past the 200-day EMA, then the situation is called a "cross." There are two types of crosses: the golden cross and the death cross. Understand both these crosses will help you plan your trading game better.

When the 50-day moving average increases above the 200-day moving average, then the situation called a golden cross and is usually considered as the sign of a bullish market. If the 50-day moving average dips below the 200-day moving average, the situation is called a death cross and is usually indicative of a bearish market.

Through such simple measures, you will be able to get a clearer idea of the market. This allows you to predict properly if the market is a bull or bear market.

Getting to know more about the 50-day and 200-day moving average is going to help you in your trades. Consider them as your trading friends, guiding you on the right path.

Chapter 7: Hot Sector Mania

Upon entering the stock market, you might find yourself wondering what sector you should tackle first. The idea of choosing the right sector becomes a daunting task because you know that there are so many options available to you.

You need to ding the right sector.

You need to find the hot sector.

Now, what is a sector?

Understanding Sectors

Think of sectors are the various sections in a library. You have the non-fiction section, fiction, biographies, history, science, and so on.

In a similar way, the stock market gets broken down into various sectors such as healthcare, energy, defense, and so on.

Typically, there are 11 major sectors that are used in stock exchanges and are the ones that comprise the economies of the world.

- Financial

- Consumer Discretionary
- Consumer Staples
- Utilities
- Energy
- Healthcare
- Telecom
- Industrials
- Technology
- Materials
- Real Estate

What exactly does recognizing a hot sector does for you?

If you can identify that one sector that seems to be on the rise, then you can invest in that sector while it is still in its growth phase. It gives traders the opportunity to work with something over the course of 3 to 12 months. Eventually, it allows them to utilize short-term trading opportunities.

How to Use Hot Sectors

Certain sectors perform better than others. Typically, the top performing sectors keep changing. If we look at the market when it is heading higher, then we need to identify which sectors is causing the increase in the market. Ideally, we should be buying stocks from the sector that is in the top position. These are usually those sectors that are performing better than the other actors in the market.

When you want to pick the hot sectors, then you have to evaluate the market from various time frames. You should not stick to just a few time frames as you might not get the most accurate results. After all, every sector shows an increase at some point in time or between a short period of time. In other words, you should be looking at sectors that are not just performing well now or a few months in the past, but also over an even longer period.

When you analyze the data, you might come across a few sectors that can be identified as the hot sectors.

Additionally, always keep a lookout on the latest news as well. You might be able to glean some valuable information and tips about what sectors have been performing really well over the course of time.

Let us look at some of the hot sectors in the market in the year 2019 so that we can get an idea of what to look out for when it comes to hot sectors.

Healthcare

The year 2019 has shown a growth in the healthcare sector. In fact, it has been performing well in the last 10 years, showing the stability of the sector. You can probably expect to use a good short-term strategy in the healthcare sector. In 2018, healthcare was the top performing sector, and while it might not have the top spot right now, it is still among the top performing sectors.

Industrial

The industrial sector is also booming. However, there are many components to the industrial sector, so choosing the right component becomes important. In this case (and for the year 2019), you should be looking at those industries that focus on pollution control, such as waste management companies. Since the concern for the planet's safety is on the rise and there is greater demand to protect the natural resources of the Earth, the demand for waste management companies is on the rise. One such example can be US Ecology (ECOL), which has been trading in the midrange for its 52nd week, maintaining consistency, and not showing any dip. Currently, the value of the stock has increased by 1.88% and is trading for $63.99.

Technology

If explosive yet volatile growth is your MO, you cannot

typically go wrong with the technology sector. You have lots of options for technology, from computing to mobile technology to space tech. You can always explore on or the other segments within the sector. In 2019, the big tech companies like Apple (AAPL) are still showing signs of growth. Currently, the stock value of Apple has increased by 4.59% and stands at $218.36. There are recommendations to go into other different segments like credit card providers and software manufacturers.

Consumer Discretionary

This sector is still showing a rise. However, be warned as many of the companies have been hit by what is known as the "Amazon effect." The online retail behemoth is still posing a threat to other companies, even though its stock value dropped by 0.37%. Currently the value of Amazon (AMZN) is $1891.53. However, there are still opportunities in the market. One only has to look at those companies that are trying to use innovating methods to lure customers to come to their stores. If you have been noticing an increase in shop visits in one of the stores despite how Amazon has affected the market, then you should consider investing in that particular store.

Let us look at some other examples of companies and sectors that were either at the top of the market or are currently topping the markets.

Dotcom Boom

Yahoo!

One of the finest examples of the dotcom boom was Yahoo! The company was initially founded by two Stanford students, David Filo, and Jerry Yang. The main idea was to create a web page that listed other websites that are interesting to the public. By the time the year 1994 arrived, Yahoo! had over hundreds of websites linked to it and was receiving an average of 1,000 page visits every week. By late 1994, the website was receiving almost 50,000 hits per day on their website. In 1996, Yahoo! had generated a revenue of $19.1 million. Their growth would continue to increase in the next year as well.

After a round of investment, Apple created its IPO. On the first day the company went public, their stocks were traded at $33 per share. They were aiming for a market capitalization of $315 million. They received a market capitalization of $866 million.

Eventually, Yahoo! entered the dotcom bubble in the years 1998-2000. After that, there were many failed investments, such as the purchase of Flickr and del.icio.us. However none of them could stop the decline in Yahoo!'s value. Once Google and Facebook entered the picture, the platform struggled to offer anything of value. The two new giants would soon dominate the market with superior offerings and better services.

The result was that Yahoo! got sold to the highest bidder, which so happens to be Verizon. The price is $4.8 billion.

If that seemed like a lot to you, then you have to consider the fact that during the dotcom bubble, Yahoo!'s value was $125 billion.

Within just 12 years, it was sold for less than 4% of its original value.

Cisco

Cisco is another company that went through the dotcom bubble. In 2011, the company announced that it would lay off 5,000 employees and even sell off a manufacturing plant in Mexico.

During the dotcom bubble, Cisco's position in the markets was so strong that it even passed Microsoft to become one of the most valuable companies in the world.

The problem with Cisco is one of growth. You see, Cisco had already reached its highest growth potential. However, investors were always seeking to see more growth. Eventually, Cisco acquired Linksys in 2003 and went on to make other acquisitions further down the line. But it was obvious. Cisco had reached its prime value during the dotcom bubble.

Eventually, the 2008 market crash hit Cisco hard. They had privately laid off 2,000 people in 2009. After trying to venture in the market for video, it made some failed investments that eventually came to haunt it in the future.

Currently, the company is losing market shares but has been managing to hold on. As of 2019, it has been showing a rise in tis stock value (by an increase of 0.27%). However, the stock itself is valued at just $56.63.

Cryptocurrency

Bitcoin

For a 6 month period in late 2017 and early 2018, it seemed impossible to go 5 minutes without hearing about Bitcoin. A meteoric rise, compared by some analysts to the Dutch tulip mania in the 17th Century, was followed by a spectacular crash in the first half of 2017. Since then, things have calmed down somewhat and the world's premiere cryptocurrency has undergone somewhat of a quiet resurgence. In 2019, Bitcoin has shown a rise of nearly 200%. One of the reasons for this is the process known as "the halvening." In this process, Bitcoin miners will only receive half rewards.

Who are Bitcoin miners? Essentially, they are groups of

people who combine their computing power in order to split the Bitcoin between the participants. This happens when the groups combined computing power is able to create new Bitcoins. These new Bitcoins will then be shared by the members of the group.

Whatever the reason may be, Bitcoin is definitely showing a rise. Whether Ethereum will soon overtake it is something that has to be seen.

Ethereum

Ethereum is the second most popular cryptocurrency in the world after Bitcoin. Some people compare the idea of buying Ethereum to purchasing a stock of Apple back when it was still growing out of a garage. expect that it might grow tremendously over the years. But due to the volatility of the market, that has to be seen.

Some analysts are predicting that that price of Ethereum will increase to nearly $2,500 this year. And this rise will continue on to the next year as well. Others are predicting that the value of Ethereum will overtake that of Bitcoin. We are still in the early stages of predictions so one cannot say what might happen by the year 2020. Others are less optimistic and have likened Ethereum to Tesla, in that it is an innovative technology, but one which may never be financially feasible.

Ripple

Ripple is a cryptocurrency that is relatively newer in the market. However, it has been showing considerable growth in recent years.

Many analysts predict that Ripple will increase its value by nearly hundredfold by the time it reaches the next bull cycle. Once again, while the cryptocurrency is definitely on the rise, it only remains to be seen if it will show a sudden upward trajectory in the future.

New Technology

Twitter

The social media company has been seeing a rise in its stock market value recently. After its daily users rose to around 139 million, the stock rose more than 5% as of June 26th. Currently, the company is showing further growth as the stock, as of July 31st, shows an increase of 4.78%. The current stock value is at $42.77.

Apple

Apple (AAPL) has always shown a growth. As we had seen earlier, the stock value of Apple has increased by 4.59% and stands at $218.36. The company has always shown improvements in the past and is continuing to do so.

Tesla

After a rough 2018, Tesla has been on the increase recently. By showing an increase of 1.53% as of July 31st, Tesla has a stock value of $245.71. With new funding from the company and its special interest in space exploration (and the trip to Mars of course), the company had garnered the attention (and even the imagination) of people around the world. Now, it only depends on how well it can perform in the coming years.

Marijuana Boom

With the laws against marijuana becoming more lenient, the industry has been seeing a boom in recent years. Here are some entities to look out for.

Canopy Growth Corporation

One of the most talked about stocks in 2018, and which began receiving mainstream coverage in 2019, the marijuana industry is seeing a boom that picked up in recent years. Despite that, you can see the effect of it on various corporations, starting with the Canopy Growth Corporation. One of the bigger players in the market, and one of the few stocks listed on the NYSE, Canopy had a rough past few months due to previous overvaluation. At the time of writing it trades at around the $32 mark and many analysts have set a buy price between $27 and $33 in the short term.

Altria

Overall, Altria Group Inc. has not been showing a growth recently. But that does not mean that it has a bad value in the market.

Formula Companies

Starbucks

The historical data of Starbucks has shown only one thing: the company has always managed to perform well and show an increase over the years. In the year 2015, the stock was traded at around $45 to $50. Now, you can see an increase in the stock value as it is now being traded at approximately $96.

In fact, one can say that this year has shown an incredible increase in the value of Starbucks. However, this growth has always been the case for the company. It has been on the rise since early 2010 and kept progressing upwards. This trend looks set to continue even after the resignation of long time CEO Howard Schultz, due to Starbucks global expansion into countries which have not traditionally had a big coffee culture like China and India. Starbucks has a unique position in this sense because they are perceived as a luxury good, but at a price which is affordable even to middle class citizens of third world countries.

Amazon

The rise of Amazon is big. In fact, currently the company has such a powerful position that it is dominating the market and overshadowing the other retail companies. The entire phenomenon has been dubbed the "Amazon effect." However, there are many companies that are adapting themselves to this effect. Those companies are making progress despite the presence of the giant retailer.

McDonald's

Another company that has been showing historical growth is McDonald's. Although the current valuation is recovering from a dip, it has always been showing growth projections from one year to the next. This makes McDonald's stock a valuable stock to have. While there has been competition from other brands such as Burger King and Wendy's (especially since the latter two brands have also been growing in popularity), McDonald's has managed to keep the top position when it comes to comparing with its competitors.

Final Words

When you look at the stock value of the above companies, then you might be thinking that there is no way that anything could affect their prices.

Take the value of Starbucks as an example. It has shown a sudden increase in value. In fact, if you look at how the value has been increasing, then one can say that there has been a spike in the value. But does that mean that you have to invest in Starbucks? Does it mean that this sudden spike is a prelude to more incredible profit margins? It does look too good to be true, right? What can you see from the historical data? One thing to remember is that whenever there has been a spike in the price value of Starbucks, there has been a decline soon.

One can never be certain if there will be a decline in the value of Starbucks. However, what you need to understand is that when something is too good to be true, it usually is.

Chapter 8: Position Entry and Exit Strategies

There are many traders who spend countless hours fine tuning their entry strategy. They reach a point where they are completely certain about their trade and are ready to make the next move. Eventually, they fail to create a successful trade and deplete their accounts soon all because they forgot to have a proper exit strategy.

Both your entry and exit strategies are important. One cannot be made without the other or else you are simply having half a plan.

Let's try to look at the basics of entering and exiting a position.

Reward and Risk Level

Since you aim to become a position trader, then you should ideally be looking (and you should be making a habit of this) at establishing a reward and risk targets. The first thing you need to do is to check out your chart and find out when the next resistance level might come into play based on the time period of your holding. This resistance level marks your reward target. We are going to look deeper into resistance and support targets. But for now, let's look at how you can establish your risk target. You simply have to choose the point that will prove that your risk has reached its limit. This point is the maximum risk that you can manage for the trade. Never try to keep your risk levels too low. You need to be realistic. Look at the funds you have and the amount you have spent on the trade. Try to evaluate your finances before deciding to choose the risk level.

Do Not Follow What Everyone Does

This is a common mistake among many traders. Whenever something happens, they begin to become part of a herd, as though being in a group gives them greater protection against the results of the trade. But that is not the case.

When a market starts correcting, you will see an increase the number of people selling the stocks. As the market dips further down, the number of people sales increases even more.

At this point, it does become a frightening prospect when you have to watch the prices of your stock dive further and further. What will happen to the stock? Are you going to face a huge loss on your investment?

Most people are afraid of loss and the eventual pain that it causes. When they see that the stock prices are going even lower, they sell because they do not want to lose any money.

Experienced traders text in a more decisive manner. They have a strategy that they have implemented, and they usually stick to that strategy. They know the risk and reward points and how much they have invested. They have performed the analysis and are prepared for the sudden shifts in the market. In short, they are not playing the short-term game and not concerned with the results in the short-term.

These experienced traders know that simply reacting to one or a few buy and sell signals is not a wise idea. They know that their strategy is based on timing and it is for that reason that they will wait longer to see further changes in the prices of the stocks.

For more historical context to this phenomena I recommend the book *A Short History of Financial Euphoria* by legendary economist JK Galbraith.

Stop-Loss Strategy

Even though you decide that you are going to wait for the long-term results of your stock, it is also prudent to have a stop-loss strategy placed just in case.

A stop-loss strategy is simply an order that you place with your broker. It states that if the stock reaches a certain point, then the broker can buy or sell the stocks, depending on your strategy.

Let us take an example to highlight the above strategy. Let us assume that you have bought stocks of Microsoft Corporation (MSFT) at $40 per share. Immediately after buying the stock, you place a stop-loss order where you mention that if the stock price falls below $35, then the broker can initiate a sell order.

One of the advantages of placing a stop-loss order is that you do not have to keep a watch on the stock on a regular basis. You know that you are not going to suffer a major loss if things don't go your way. In fact, you are probably going to be safe (or safe as possible) with your investments.

Scaling Your Exit Strategies

When a new trade moves into a profit, then you can try to scale up your stop-loss order. This way, you are following the profit trend and at the same time, you are building confidence in trading. If you always keep a low stop-loss order and the price reaches that level, then you have missed an opportunity to make a profit. As you go along with the price increase, you are improving your chances of making a profit.

Stick to Your Plan

Make no mistake — your trading success depends on your ability to stick to your trading plan. Never deviate from that plan because every other decision might seem like the right thing to do. However, they are not the decisions that you had planned to take earlier. So, do not go down a path you are unfamiliar with. Besides, you are more concerned with the long-term effects of your trade. Do not let short-term changes affect the way you think about your trades and your plan.

Support and Resistance

Examine a chart. See the rise in the price of a stock. You will notice it rising until it reaches a certain point. After that, it begins to take a reverse course, falling. That point at which it pulls back is called the resistance.

In the same way, the lowest point that the price reaches before it begins to go back up is called the support.

But how do you trade with support and resistance levels?

Here are a few ways to use support and resistance in your trading.

Profit-Taking Strategies

Majors and Minors

In most cases, you might find that there are minor support levels on the charts. Only, these support levels are likely to be broken.

For example, let us assume that the price of the stock Apple Inc (AAPL) is dropping. It will reach a point after which it will bounce back. That point is called the minor support level. After a certain increase, the stock price will dip again. This time, it might pass your minor support levels.

When you use a minor support level, you gain more insights about the stock. If the price continues its downward trajectory, then you know that the stock's trend is intact. This will allow you to make some decisions. However, if the price bounces back up, then you know that a range could be developing. This range can give you the support and resistance levels of the stock price.

In case of the major level, we are looking at stocks that suddenly turn in the opposite direction after reaching a point. For example, if the price has been seeing an upward trend and suddenly starts going in a downward trend, then that point from which the price bounced is known as the major resistance level.

What's the difference between a minor level and a major level?

In a minor level, the price usually breaks through that level and continues onwards. In a major level, the price bounces and start going in the opposite direction.

Range Trading

Traders may sometimes choose to engage in range training, which takes place between the support and resistance levels. One of the things you have to remember is that the levels of support and resistance are not always perfect lines. Sometimes, they bounce off a particular area. It is also important to know that the support and resistance levels are not exact numbers. They are just levels that help you understand where you can find the support and resistance.

When the market is in a range, the traders are on the lookout for long entries were the prices bounce off a support level and short entries where the prices bounce off resistance levels.

Trendline Strategy

In this strategy, one uses the trendline as a support or resistance level. All you have to do is identify two or more highs in a downward trend of the price. This will allow you to create a support trendline. Similarly, if you can identify two or more lows in the upward trend of the price, then you will be able to draw a resistance trendline.

So, once you have these trendlines, then you should ideally be looking for entries along the trendlines. You should initiate a buy order along the support trendline and a sell order along the resistance trendline. This is because you are following certain trends and improving your odds of trading at a profit.

The False Breakout

The name "false breakout" is used appropriately and describes the situation perfectly. What it means is that the price of a stock was heading towards a breakout but failed to go beyond a particular level. This initiates a false breakout situation. False breakouts are an important indicator in trading because when a false breakout occurs, then it either means that the price is about to change direction or that there will be an occurrence of a trend.

A false breakout is also often described by the market as a form of deception. The reason is that the price looked like it was about to breakout but simply rebounded and headed in the opposite direction, making certain traders believe that it was going to breakout but instead, they get deceived by the price movement.

So, why do false breakouts happen?

Usually, it is the result of novice traders or those with "weak hands" (a market term for people who do not take any risks) enter the market at a point where they feel that they are safe to enter. This means that they enter the market when it is already headed towards a particular direction and then try to make a prediction about a breakout from a particular support or resistance level too quickly.

For professional traders, however, this is an opportunity. How can one trade during a false breakout?

Step 1: Look For a Swing Low

The first thing that you have to focus on is identifying the swing low, which is simply the low price movement of your stock. When you look at a chart, you will notice that the price usually moves in waves. When the price moves to certain low points within those waves and then bounces back up, then those points are termed as swing low.

The swing low lines are not necessarily the support line that we are looking for. This is because they often indicate a false breakout line.

However, swing lows can be used by traders who are holding a long position to find their stop-loss order.

What it tells us is that if there are multiple swing lows after a downward trend has been continuing for long, then that can indicate that a market bottom is about to take place. Traders can use this information to predict where they can set up their stop-loss or modify their strategy to meet the trend taking place.

Step 2: Below Swing Low

At this point, you should ideally wait for the stock to go below the swing low. In other words, you have to make sure that the price has gone below the false breakout line. Once the price reaches beyond this point, you can make your move.

At this point, traders can place a stop-loss order below the swing low in case there is a reversal in the price, and they would like to pull out fast. However, you are now waiting for the price to rise.

Step 3: Above Swing Low

In the next step, you are now waiting for the stock to go above the swing low. As it continues its upwards trend, you can stop-loss to go higher after each successful swing low. This way, you are moving up with the price. What you are doing in this scenario is that you are waiting for the stock to return to the upside.

When you have mastered the above steps, then you will have a clear idea of how you would like to buy and sell the stock. This will also help you manage your losses better and create an effective trading strategy.

Volatility Contraction

Trading with volatility contractions are an important way to trade stocks because you are using trends to work with your stocks.

Here is the truth of the market: it moves from a situation of high volatility to a situation of low volatility without any warning. In other words, the volatility is never constant. It always fluctuates based on market conditions and other factors.

When you are trading, you should usually enter into a period of low volatility. The reason is that the range on the charts get smaller as the volatility contracts.

Let's put it this way: When the market is at low-volatility, then you can easily predict the range and set up your stop-loss. In this manner, you have the advantage of setting up a tighter stop-loss. You can use this stop-loss on a big position size and still keep your risk as minimal as possible.

Setting Up Stop-Loss Properly

Nobody likes to lose money.

That is obvious, and it applies to everyone. The thing is, you cannot always avoid losing money in trading. However,

Position Trading

what you can control is the amount of money that you lose.

One of the biggest challenges that traders face is deciding where they would like to set up their stop loss order. Should they take more risks, or should they try and minimize the risk?

A stop-loss order, as we have seen earlier, is simply an order for your broker to sell your socks should the price of that stock falls below a particular point.

Let us assume that you have stocks worth $30 with you. You decide that your stop-loss point should be placed where the price drops by 10%. This means that you are going to place your stop-loss order at $30 minus the 10% criteria that you placed. This would be at $27.

Another strategy that you can apply is place a time period for your stop-loss. If your stock is not sold within a particular time period, they the broker will initiate a sale for you.

- The first thing that you are going to do is calculate the price of the stop-loss point. For this, you have to look at your chart and identify ranges of your stock over the course of therapist six months or more. Make sure you research the stock properly so that you have acclimated to its high points and low points.

- Now, calculate the median (or the midpoint line) on the chart.

- From that midpoint line, set up a stop-loss order anywhere between 4-7% from the median.

That is all there is to it. Make sure that you are well-versed with the trends of your chart before you begin to set up the stop-loss order.

When Do You Take Profits?

This is an important question that everyone asks themselves when they are trading. At what point should you consider taking in the profits? Do you have to take them when you see the first sign of an upward direction of the price of your stock? Should you wait longer?

Everyone likes to earn as much profit as possible. But the best way to improve your portfolio is to use the 20-25% rule. Here is how it works.

When you notice that the price is going in an upward trend, then allow it to go in that direction. When the price point has advanced by 20% or 25%, then you can initiate a sell order and take your profit. But why choose to stick to just 20% or 25% and not go higher? In many cases, the markets might hit corrections when the stock has advanced anywhere from 20% to 40%. When you apply the 20-25% rule, then you are allowing the price to go into the upward direction as much as possible before you pull out with a profit.

Chapter 9: Money Management

You are now used to fundamental and technical analysis. You can read the market and you know how to place your stop-loss orders. You are pretty much ready to take on the market and get your first profit!

However, there is one more important factor that you have to take into consideration before you begin to trade. You need to know how to manage your risk.

Most people do not ponder about how they should go about managing their risk. They think that as long as they are confident about their entry points, performed all the necessary research, and set up their stop-loss points, then they are good to go.

You need to know how to manage your risks or else everything you have learned until this point becomes rather moot.

Let us start off with the risk-and-reward assessment.

Risk/Reward Assessment

This assessment helps you understand just how much reward you are going to gain for the risk that you are placing in your trade.

Typically, the risk reward ratio is set at 2:1 so that you are compensated well for the risk that you have taken.

For instance, you are interested in the stock of a company called ARC. ARC is now trading at $30 from a previous trade price of $35. It has fallen by $5. You now have $600 with you to spend on this investment. After you have conducted your research and analysis, you believe that the stock price will go back up to $35 soon. You decide that you are going to buy 20 shares of the product. (With an investment of $600 and with $30 per share, you can buy a total of 20 shares).

Now that you have made the decision. You wait for the stock price to rise up. Let us assume that the stock price goes up to $35. Essentially, you have made a profit of $5 for each of the 20 shares you have with you. That is a total of $100.

You know that you are likely to get a profit of $100. Consider that you have put your stop-loss at $25. If you calculate that, then your risk is now $100. So, your risk is $100 while your reward is $100. This gives reward to risk ratio of 1:1. That is not ideal at all.

Now, let's say that we decide to change our risk amount. Rather than going for $25, we choose to go for $27.5 instead. Our risk now is only $2.5 per share or a total of $50. Our new reward to risk ratio is now 100/50. The new reward to risk ratio is 2:1. This seems more ideal to us at this point and we shall go ahead and take this reward to risk ratio.

Managing Trade Size

One of the most important decisions you will make in trading involves how much your trade size is going to be. Usually, you are going to use a percentage or dollar limit for each of the trades you are going to make.

Most traders choose not to risk more than 1% of their account on a single trade. Let's say that you have $10,000 in your account. With that amount, you are not going to risk more than $100 per trade. If you like, you can always go below that 1%, but you are going to decide never to go above the 1% mark.

Due to brokerage fees, this rule can be increased to 2% per trade if your total trading account is at $10,000 or less. But as a rule, you should never risk more than 2% of your account in a single trade.

This percentage rule that you set up will become your trade size.

Trading Journal

You can manage your performance by keeping a trade

journal. Using this journal, you will be able to evaluate your past performance and then learn from your mistakes. When you want to succeed in the world of trading, then you need to have a lot of planning and understanding of the market. However, you may never know which of you plans had worked and which ones did not if you do not maintain a trade journal.

When you have a trading journal, you record each trade you have made along with all the details you can add about that trade. These details can then be reviewed in the future before you go on to start another trade. By doing so, you will not follow the same strategy if it had failed. On the other hand, if your previous strategy was a success, then you can continue to use it or find ways to modify it so it could produce better yields.

Additionally, when you have a trader journal, you become more and more analytical. You learn from each trade you make. This helps you remove the emotion out of the equation. You begin to rely on raw data and information. You ignore the sudden impulses you receive when you are faced with a certain scenario. All you have to do is refer to your journal and see if you have faced the situation in the past.

Using Sample Trade Examples With Real Numbers

When you can learn from examples, then you may find yourself having more clarity when dealing with trades. However, do not choose to have an example that you cannot apply in real life. If you have real examples with real numbers, they are basically learning from a trade that has occurred in real life. This helps you find trades that are similar to yours or even learn some effective strategies from past trades.

When you use arbitrary numbers, then you are not sure if the strategy employed in that example will work or not since it hasn't actually happened.

Using real examples gives you confidence. In the world of trading confidence, it is the key to taking important decisions.

Consider the Golden Rule

Remember that even professional traders face losses. No one is immune to the effects of the stock market. Anybody can win or lose in trading.

What separates the novice from the experts, though, is the ability to handle the losses. When a new trader experiences loss, he or she then either starts paying too much attention to that loss or impulsively decides to make up for the loss by creating another mistake.

Expert traders, on the other hand, do not let their emotions get the better of them. They are focused. They analyze their losses and see what went wrong. Then, they ask themselves the following questions:

- Can the trade be salvaged?
- Should they return to the same trade?
- what have they done that led them to the loss?
- What can they do different?
- Was their strategy flawed? If so, is there something they should do to change their tactics?

They know that they can recover, if only they apply their logic to learn from their past losses.

Chapter 10: 7 Psychological Traps Every Trader Faces

Trading can be an intense scenario. The people who are not used to the psychological experiences of trading might not be prepared to face all the various psychological traps we might experience while trading. Let us look at some of these traps.

Trap #1: Confirmation Bias

We are always under the impression that we are people who are open to criticism and contradictory views. Unfortunately, psychology has a much different viewpoint than that. You see, we are usually biased. We look for information that supports our viewpoints and tend to ignore that information that contradicts our viewpoints.

This phenomenon is called "confirmation bias," and it is quite dangerous in the world of trading. We refuse to believe in the facts that seem to oppose the views that we have set up for ourselves. For example, whenever we suffer a loss, we might believe that there is a chance to bounce back. We become emotional after the loss that we fail to see the logical path: that we simply have to move on from that trade. However, our confirmation bias forces us to look for any bit of information that supports our theory that we are right and that the stock is capable of returning our investment.

In the world of trading, this is not always the case.

You need to be open to the idea that sometimes, the stocks have not worked out in your favor. You need to be able to accept the fact that you could be wrong about something.

Trap #2: Sunk-Cost Fallacy

Nobody likes to see all their hard work get flushed down the proverbial toilet. It is heartbreaking, disappointing, and sometimes a tough pill to swallow.

Defeats are part of the learning process. Through defeats, you understand what should be done and what should be avoided. They can guide you along the right part.

However, you can only learn from defeats if you allow them to teach you something. Many people delve into their defeats and refuse to acknowledge them.

This is what happens in a sunk-cost fallacy. In this fallacy, people continue a particular act, decision, or behavior because they have invested considerable money, effort, or time. By doing so, people refuse to let go of such things, even if they are only going to cause more harm.

For example, let us imagine that Trader A has used a particular strategy for a trade. He or she has invested time and money to make sure that the trade reaps profitable results. Sadly, the trade ends up hitting a low, and Trade A realizes that the only thing he or she has gained is a losing trade. Rather than accepting the reality, Trader A continues to invest even more money and time into the trade.

Don't let that happen to you. Again, a loss is a loss.

Trap #3: Situational Blindness

Situational blindness is the distant cousin of confirmation bias. Sometimes, people may be choosing to willingly block out information from other sources, thinking that if they face those sources, then they might only receive bad news.

Whether you receive good or bad news, make sure that you are always getting your information right. Bad news is not the end of your trading life. However, ignoring bad news might just be.

Trap #4: Relativity Trap

Everyone has a unique psychological print. It's almost like a fingerprint, unique to each and every person. For this reason, not everyone might be looking at a trade using the same expectations, ideas, strategies, and information.

When you are entering a trade, therefore, make sure you keep your goals, available funds, and information at hand. Do not listen to people around you because they think they have a better idea for your trade.

It is alright to take valuable tips and information from veterans. In the end, you are the one who controls your trade.

Trap #5: Irrational Exuberance Trap

The past is not an indication of the future. Just because something has happened in the past does not mean that it will, with certainty, happen in the future. Believing that is putting yourself in a false sense of confidence. In fact, it can also be a situation of overconfidence, preventing you from looking at a trade with rational thought.

Trap #6: Superiority Trap

There is no limit to learning. Keep this in mind as you begin and continue trading. Always consider yourself as a student.

Often, you might come across traders who think that they know better than most people. In fact, just because they saw a YouTube video made by someone who has a "secret technique" or recently came across a book with insider tips, they feel that they know better than even veteran traders.

Do not let the feeling of superiority overwhelm you. Even if you think that you have learned everything there is to know about trading, keeping your focus on the information in front of you, listen to what other traders are saying with an open mind. Never forget as well that the more you learn, the more you earn.

Trap #7: Texas Sharpshooter Fallacy

Imagine a cowboy getting ready to shoot the side of a barn. His hands are poised on his revolvers. His face has a grim expression, like he's about the destroy the barn itself with his bullets. Quick as lightning, he whips out his revolvers and fires one shot after another into the side of the barn until his chambers are empty. He looks at the results and notices that the bullet holes are all over the wall. It looks like he is not a good shot after all, but what he does next is quite perplexing.

He walks up to the wall, takes out a chalk, draws a circle around a random cluster of bullet holes and then exclaims, "See? I have hit bullseye!"

He hadn't actually hit bullseye. He created a bullseye

himself. He created order around a random distribution of bullet holes.

As humans, we do not like to feel that things are arbitrary. We love to place order on chaos. Unfortunately, this might pose a problem to us because we start creating connections between a random assortment of facts, even when no such connections exist.

When you are trading and you notice a collection of information, do not attempt to draw conclusions by yourself. Do not make connections when there are not. Just like the bullet holes, do not group together random information and think that you may have found a valuable secret.

Always follow the facts. If you spot something, use your due diligence to find out more about it.

Never assume anything. It is fun to watch characters in movies look really smart by finding a pattern in a cluster of information. But that is not how real life works. Even veterans do not try to find patterns. They simply follow the information and see where it leads them.

Conclusion

Position trading is a long-term strategy.

That is something you have to keep in mind before you enter into position trading. You see, many people forget the fact that they are going to have to wait for months to see the progress their trade makes. They get so caught up in the small details or the short-term changes of their stock. This compels them to make some rather hasty decisions.

The main reason for choosing position trading is that it is supposed to add less stress into your life. What's the point of worrying about the small details and increasing your stress levels? Sure, you do have to monitor your trades every day, but you are not concerned about all the changes that happen every day.

Leave the daily strategy for the day traders.

Remember that even though position trading is a long-term strategy, it is is much safer than other forms of trading. In most trading forms, you are looking at changes that happen every single day. If you miss out on one single piece of information or trend change, then you are going to miss out on an opportunity to make profits.

The most important factor for you to remember is that you

need to learn everything you can from this book so you can strengthen your foundation. By going through the basics, you are creating an understanding of the market. As you deal with the market, you build upon the foundation you have laid down, getting better with every trade that you make.

One of the biggest advantages is that you can get involved with position trading while having a full-time job as well. This is ideal for people who do not want to give up on their career for trading. They simply have to spend 30 minutes every day to look through your stock and see if you need to make any small adjustments.

Always be prepared before any trade. Understand your trade size. Check your stop-loss and other strategies. It is only when you are sure of everything that you should decide to enter into a trade.

Do not let your emotions overwhelm you. Keep your mind focused on the information you have, not on the emotions you feel.

Happy trading!

Printed in France by Amazon
Brétigny-sur-Orge, FR